Cont

CW01099622

FOREWORD by Rob Bailey

I firmly believe the North Staffordshire and South Cheshire League to be one of the finest in the country. It has given so many cricketers a springboard to the highest level of the game.

For me, playing in the North Staffordshire and South Cheshire League at Knypersley as a young cricketer with team mates like Bob Cooke, Peter Eyres and David Ling was so valuable. They were all former first class cricketers and I was given the opportunity to play with these high quality sportsmen by our captain, Ken Young.

My congratulations to the North Staffordshire and South Cheshire League on your fifty not out. Long may you continue to be up there with the best in the land carrying on the fine traditions of developing cricketers for the future.

Robert John Bailey

Rob was born in Biddulph in 1963, he played first class cricket for England (4 test caps and 4 ODI Caps), Derbyshire and Northamptonshire during the period 1982 to 2001. Rob joined the full list of first class umpires in 2006.

CRICKET IN NORTH STAFFORDSHIRE AND SOUTH CHESHIRE
- THE EARLY YEARS
By Tony Loffill

The game of cricket has long been mainlined into our DNA. If we are to believe one obscure historic source it was being played back in the early 14th century in the time of King Edward the Second – perhaps not the best role model for modern cricketers to adopt... What is more certain is that by the 18th century the game was established in Sussex and Kent, whence it moved to London where it was taken up by the aristocracy to become a fashionable dimension of society and where large sums were bet on the outcome of matches – one activity which has come full circle today.

How and why the game moved North is a story largely lost and forgotten. It did eventually find its way to Mercia, to a country bounded by the Trent, the Weaver, the Dove, and the Dane, to the smoky burgeoning towns of the Potteries, to the brooklands of their rural surroundings, to the lush pastures of Cheshire (considered unkindly by its Staffordshire neighbours to have the shape of an oatcake) and to the windy eastern Moorlands.

The Six Towns (Arnold Bennett seemingly unable to count beyond five) took up the game with enthusiasm. Clubs were formed in fields among the bottle kilns, the brickworks, the canals, the pit shafts, the iron foundries, the grey church towers, the chapels: the unique landscape of a place "where beauty was achieved and none saw it".

To the men who toiled long hours in the smoke-choked towns cricket gave a pause for them to feel the sun on their brow, the wind on their cheek. Their country cousins had no easier lives: hunger and dirt were as much a part of their daily existence as it was of their urban neighbours. They too still sought rare moments of leisure playing the game on their village pastures.

Early references to the game locally are scant indeed; although Rode Park lays claim to an 18th century reference. Was this perhaps some Cheshire gentleman anxious to show that he could keep up with the fashion of the day by introducing this southern game to the wild North? What is certain is that by the middle of the 19th century communities all over the area were forming clubs and playing competitive cricket, almost none of which, frustratingly, was ever recorded for posterity.

The great revolution for local cricket in the 19th century appeared in the form of the railways. Teams whose horizons stretched no further than a journey on a wagon were suddenly able to take the train to find opponents further afield. Cricket was on the move. The idea of forming groups in which to compete slowly developed. It was a long process. Many clubs, particularly those in village communities, were content to play their games on a traditional ad hoc basis. But by the 1970s the writing was on the wall for friendly Saturday cricket as clubs opted for the practicality of an organised, structured system. Friendly cricket is for evenings and Sundays now.

To appreciate the structure and governance of the NSSC and to perhaps also give a nod of respect to the cricketers of ours who have gone before, it might be fitting to identify a few of the leagues whose values and traditions have come down to us. There are surprisingly many and this cannot claim to be an exhaustive list. The Cheshire League, The Cheshire County League, the Cheshire Club Conference, the Cheshire Cricket Alliance, the Cheshire Competition, the North Staffs Combination, the North Staffs League, the North Staffs and District League, the Kidsgrove League, the Kidsgrove and District League, the Stone League, the Stafford Club Championship, the Birmingham Combination, the Stafford Championship, the South Moorlands League, the Churnet Valley League, the Scot Hay Midweek League, the War Workers League, the Fenton League and the Tunstall and District League. Some of these are still very much alive. although most have gone now. Yet all, in greater or lesser fashion, have helped shape our league as it is today.

One league that perhaps deserves a special mention is the only recently vanished South Cheshire League. This was an ambitious step made in the 1970s to bring league status to smaller clubs who had lived on a diet of friendly cricket and who were recognising the trend to organised managed competitions. Teams were drawn from Staffordshire, Cheshire and Shropshire and in the 20 or so years of the league's existence village clubs acquired the skills and tastes for league cricket which enabled many of them to progress to the higher ECB model. What marked out the South Cheshire was its excellent management structure: local cricket was seen to need careful overseeing and hands-on care. The driving force behind the league was Derek Worthy who's other claim to fame was that one day while playing at Over Peover he died at the wicket. Luckily he chose for his demise a well heeled village whose cricket ground was surrounded by the houses of many Manchester consultants, one of whom hurried out to bring Derek back to life. When asked later what he'd seen during his brief absence the answer was typically succinct. "Nothing". No more questions.

Just as the traditions of the former leagues have combined to give shape to the NSSC so too have the cricketers who have gone before – some of them truly great players, Arthur Shrewsbury, the cricketer W G Grace admired before all others, appeared for Leek in the 19th century. But his cricket belonged to Nottingham. One who was home grown, a true native, was the game's greatest ever bowler, S.F (Sydney) Barnes, born in Staffordshire in 1873, who during

the winter of 1912 during an hour and a half's bowling on a perfect Australian wicket took five wickets for nine runs.. Sadly for the first class game Barnes forsook the county and test arenas and earned a rich living in the leagues: one of the initial cricketing mercenaries. Forty one years after his feats in Australia he came out to bowl the honorary first ball of the Minor Counties versus the Australians match at Hanford and belied his age with a ball that spun off a perfect length.

Records of the years between the wars are alas sparse and not well kept so that many of the deeds of those times when league cricket flourished, often before crowds of considerable size, are confined to the archives. One name that has survived is that of Aaron Lockett, a considerable cricketer, born in Audley but playing his local cricket at nearby Bignall End. His finest match was in 1928 when playing for the Minor Counties against a West Indian team fielding the mighty Learie Constantine. He scored 158. He broke many hearts at Bignall End when he defected to Old Hill; but after some seasons there and in the Lancashire leagues he came back to his native heath. He became a first class umpire for a couple of seasons and continued playing competitive cricket till the age of 69... He was a colossus in the local game for many years. His skills were not restricted to cricket. In his youth he turned out both for Port Vale and Stoke City: where his loyalties were it is now impossible to guess.

Men who played football and cricket to a high level were a common feature until fairly recent days when football league managers became jealous of the fitness of their highly paid players and forbade them participating in the dangerous game of cricket. To quote Dennis Smith, the "iron man" in his days at the Victoria Ground and no mean cricketer himself, "We all loved our cricket .Peter Dobing was good enough to play for Lancashire seconds and a lot of us enjoyed playing for local clubs in the summer. The football seasons were shorter then as well." Albert Leake and Basil Hayward were two of the Vale Valiants who were also performers of note, the latter representing his county. Tony Allen, Stoke City's international left back was a doughty performer for spectral Caverswall where history hovers; John Farmer, a safe pair of hands, played with Leek; Denis Herod, another goalkeeper, was at Audley; Phil Sproson (ex- Vale) chose Whitmore, Wilf Hall turned out for Fenton. There is, alas, no record of Sir Stanley having tried his hand at the league game. He is reputed to have been a dazzling wicket keeper for his Wellington Road school; who knows what story we might be telling if he'd turned to cricket!

The other commanding local figure of the time, on both sides of the Second World War, was Stan Crump. He represented his county from 1930 until 1960 and was a member of one of the most prolific families in local cricket, including

Freddie "Nobby" Steele, the Steele brothers, David and John, Brian Crump and Jeremy Snape.

During the years of the Second World War clubs struggled to survive and only those who could call on men in reserved occupations could hope to play regular cricket. Some interesting travellers passed by the way then, blown around by the fortunes of war. Perhaps the most famous was Fred Root who had opened the bowling for England in 1926 when England won the Ashes back from Australia after twenty long years. It was his unfortunate fate to be replaced by debutant Harold Larwood who went on to become England's most fearsome fast bowler.

League cricket was quick to revive after the war. The population had been starved of good sport and flocked in great numbers to see the cricket where old rivalries were quickly resumed .Games were comprehensively covered in the local press. Some of the names to note in those early peacetime seasons were of men who made sure the traditional high standards were resumed and maintained: Shardlow, Bailey, Boon, Taylor and Burgess; and obviously many more too numerous to mention here - except perhaps the name of E.D.Dennis of Longton who symbolised in many respects the best values of our leagues. A Potteries solicitor, diminutive in stature, he overcame a potentially crippling handicap by keeping wicket expertly enough to become the regular keeper for his county.

In 1946 the county was represented at Test level by J.T Ikin who travelled on Wally Hammond's tour to Australia and New Zealand. He acquitted himself well in a losing cause on a difficult trip. He was the first of a succession of Test and international players produced by the leagues and most are listed in the features written on the clubs; but it is of interest to see them called to mind separately.

Barnes and Ikin were the first of a select band who learned their cricket in the company of our league players. In 1966 the next local player took his place in the Test match scene. Ken Higgs (Sandyford) was, in the words of Colin Bateman, "a fine medium fast bowler" who took 71 wickets at Test level at an average of just over 20, remarkable figures in an age when batsmen held sway. Ken was also involved in a last wicket stand of 128 with John Snow, the English record which still stands for England in this country. He then, despite being named as a Wisden Cricketer of the Year, as Bateman says "inexplicably fell out of favour with the selectors" Another cricketing mystery never satisfactorily explained.

Dominic Cork (Betley and Porthill Park), in a colourful career, took 131 wickets for his country. He exploded on to the scene in 1995 taking seven West Indian wickets for 43 in the best figures achieved by a debutant. He followed this up with a sensational Sunday morning hat trick and then for good measure a half century in the fourth Test. He was immediately christened the "new Botham" and his annus mirabilis was crowned with a Cricketer of the Year award. His career had its ups and downs. He twice moved counties, first to Lancashire, then to Hampshire. In 2010 he switched sports to "Dancing on Ice" without success. He is now a sports commentator for Sky.

Bob Taylor (Bignall End) was truly the prince of wicket keepers. He grew up in the shadow of the Victoria Ground where, like Garth Crooks after him, he honed his football and cricket skills on the club car park. He did have thoughts of pursuing a career at Vale Park but concentrated on his cricket making his first appearance for Staffordshire at the age of 15 where he was mistaken for a young spectator. Known as "chat" to his teammates for his liking to keep the conversation going at the wicket, he had a long association with the England team, making his debut in 1970 and playing his final game only in 1983. He had the misfortune to come up against Alan Knott, seen as a superior batsman, and this curtailed his international appearances. He was undoubtedly the best wicket keeper of his time. When Wisden elected him a Cricketer of the Year in 1977 they paid him a rich compliment - "his artistry behind the stumps has long illumined even the darkest hours of Derbyshire cricket."

John Morris (Crewe), an exciting and highly gifted batsman, won three caps for his country but will be best remembered for his role as co pilot to David Gower flying over an up country game in Australia, a stunt which badly backfired. The England management was not amused and fined him heavily and this unfortunate episode probably ended the hopes of a Test career of a man named by Wisden as "a talented and potentially destructive batsman".

Kim Barnett (Leek) made early progress in the game. At the age of only 15 he appeared both for Northamptonshire and Warwickshire Second Elevens. He was appointed captain of Derbyshire at the age of 22, gradually developing the dancing technique at the wicket, moving early to bring him closer to the pitch of

the ball. This style, though unorthodox, obviously worked for him. He developed a taste for big scores and this brought him to the attention of selector David Graveney who described an innings of 175 against Gloucestershire as one of the finest innings he had ever seen. His appearances for his country would without doubt have exceeded the four he made but for his decision to join the ill-considered Mike Gatting tour to South Africa in 1988. He was a Wisden Cricketer of the Year in 1988 and is still active in the game opening the batting for Hem Heath.

David Steele (Sneyd) was destined to become probably the widest known of our iconic players. Grey haired and bespectacled, he was an unlikely selection to face rampant Australian in 1975. Dubbed by the media "the bank clerk who went to war" and greeted by Rodney Marsh on his way out to bat at Lord's with "They've sent out Groucho Marx", (he was lucky not to be timed out as he had lost his way from the dressing room on to the field of play) he had such a successful series that he was elected BBC Sports Personality of the Year in the same year. The following season, David's benefit year, a local butcher offered him a lamb chop for every run he made. An expensive gesture: David scored 1756 lamb chops that year, filled his freezer and was named a Wisden Cricketer of the Year.

He was one of many local players who sought a first class future in Derbyshire, as did eventually Rob Bailey (Knypersley) who spent most of his career with Northamptonshire. Just like the Steeles and the Crumps. Rob is a member of one of Staffordshire's famous cricket dynasties being closely related to the Boon family, several of whom played for the county. Rob must be counted one of the unlucky Test players. Selected on the tour of the Caribbean in 1988-89 he took his place in the Test team facing the mighty battery of West Indian fast bowlers. He was given out – some say with the encouragement of Viv Richards – caught at the wicket off his hip. One of the all time shocking decisions. Although he went on to make a dogged 42 in Antigua against the same attack he was never picked again despite, in the words of Michael Henderson "generally regarded as being one of the finest men to play county cricket in the last thirty years". His consolation is that he has

become Staffordshire's most successful umpire, destined, if he so chooses, to reach the very top of his profession.

The most recent of our local prodigies to reach the top echelon is Danni Wyatt, the off spinning all rounder, the treasure of Whitmore Cricket club and the first of our women players to play for their country. Cricket has come a long way since 1963 when women's cricket was not considered as a serious pastime. A powerful argument against cricket's conservative reputation is to see how the game has moved with the times; and what was once a game played by only a handful of women has now reached a status unimaginable fifty years ago. The women now represent a highly respected element in our game and Danni serves as a shining inspiration for others to follow.

There is another of our league's sons who can justly claim that fortune has not always favoured him. Alan Richardson of Little Stoke would surely have secured a place in Test history had he not suffered a series of injuries. Fulfilment did come his way towards his final days on the field, when he gave a series of master classes in fast medium seam bowling which to the pleasure of all his supporters earned him the deserved accolade of one of Wisden's Five Cricketers of the Year.

What all these players have in common is the debt they owe to the local leagues, which by the examples and high standards set, nurtured and developed them.

In view of the numbers of quality performers who come out of our league it follows that the question of first class status arises. Why are Staffordshire and Cheshire not members of the first class fraternity? The counties are large and populous enough. Northamptonshire, Derbyshire and Leicestershire are just three county clubs which survive in small surroundings. It could be that Staffordshire remained a minor county because of the political and linguistic differences between the north and south of the county (Mistake a Potter for a Black Country man at your peril.) Cheshire's population has expanded greatly over the last fifty years. Whatever the reasons Staffordshire, Cheshire and Shropshire clubs have been a rich treasure house readily plundered by the big county beasts. The full list of local talent obliged to seek cricketing fame and fortune in other counties would take up more space than is available in this publication: just the most notable few will have to suffice.

One of the most remarkable family trees in the area can date its formidable line from Stan Crump of Chell. His son Brian was a successful all rounder with Northamptonshire over many seasons. Brian's cousins, David and John Steele, both had long and successful careers, the latter with Leicestershire and Glamorgan. John has recently retired from a second career as a first class umpire. Kidsgrove's Jeremy Snape, from the same family, enjoyed a distinguished career with several counties.

Norton's Peter Gibbs, after a fruitful sequence of seasons at Derbyshire, exchanged the game for the theatre and the pen. Andrew Brassington and Phil Bainbridge, Sneyd boys both, migrated to Gloucestershire and Durham.

There remains one hero to be remembered. Albert Lightfoot of Woore. A consistent performer with bat and ball for Northamptonshire, he found his way into the archives with a partnership in company with the Test player Subba Row when, at The Oval in 1958, they amassed 376 runs for the sixth wicket against the mighty Surrey attack, a record which stood for over fifty years.

Who do we so often neglect in our recollections of our game? Why, the umpires and the ladies. The umpires, those hardy, long suffering philosophical men who stand long hours in all weathers for little or no reward. It was once allowed to ask for volunteers from the crowd to do the job. That wouldn't do now. Our umpires, worthy men that they are, have these days pretty well to be in possession of a Harvard degree in astrophysics before they are deemed fit to stand. Umpires used to travel with their clubs. "Who takes most wickets for your team? "might be the question. "Why, old chap, I do." Now the men in the white coats have joined the ranks of the independent professionals. Man is born to sin and error but our umpires "wear the robes of wisdom and virtue and law and infallibility all rolled into one" Where would we be without them?

No story of our league would be properly complete without recognition of the role played by the women. The game simply could not be run without them.

"Why we'd have to get our own teas and wash our own clothes" was once the cry that would have gone up. The man who made such utterances today would have to watch his step. They play a vital role in the running of our clubs. No role is beyond them.

One of their traditional areas of expertise is found in the scorebox where along with the retired players, the schoolboys, the ones who fail to catch the selectors' eye, they join the long line of notchers, chalkers, scorebook keepers and computer operators who over the ages have shouted "bowler's name" (often several times) and huddled close at the end of play to find that missing leg-bye.

For some the act of scoring has become an art form. Lester Meredith and Stuart Foster remain two of the longest serving scorers in the league. On such folk does our enjoyment and pleasure rest.

In the fifties, in the years running up to the formation of the present North Staffs and South Cheshire League, the reputation of the cricket in the North West Midlands grew apace. No longer was quality league cricket seen to be restricted to Yorkshire and Lancashire. Ambitious club chairmen, anxious to attract international names to adorn the local clubs, spared no effort or expense in searching for the best. Players of Test status soon realised that the standard of play in the league was as high as anywhere in the country and that their reputations were not at risk in coming to the NSSC.

Famous names soon signed up. They make up a glistering list, adding up to well over a hundred names over the last sixty years or so. Norton captured the biggest prizes with Garfield Sobers, Jim Laker and Frank Worrell (not at the same time – not even Norton could manage that). "Sonny" Ramadhin brought his mysteries to Nantwich and then Ashcombe Park who also employed pipe smoking Vanburn Holder. Tino Best and Ottis Gibson found their way to Leek. Chell opted for raw speed: Wes Hall and Roy Gilchrist.

Knypersley's ground saw the birth of two distinguished careers. Frank "Typhoon" Tyson was a young pro for the club and is said to have begun his run up from behind the sight screen. In the same era Bob Appleyard made his debut for Yorkshire Second Eleven in a Minor Counties game and took fifteen wickets. The following year he took 200 first class wickets, an amazing feat, impossible in present day cricket. Bob, soon to turn 90, is still a regular and critical visitor to Headingley and Scarborough to watch his old county. He remembers Knypersley with great affection. "It changed my life". Tyson and Appleyard played leading roles in the victorious Ashes series in Australia in 1954-55.

In their good days Sneyd could boast Ken Shuttleworth and Vince Lindo; Peter Such turned up at Cheadle and Jeff Cook at Caverswall; Dean Headley was an eye catching acquisition by Leycett. John Ward, one of the few cricketers to be sent off in a first class match, played at Bignall End. Little Stoke went for spin in the shape of Mushtaq Ahmed and Shahid Afridi. All these together with a host of high class performers from all over the cricketing world who by their example and inspiration raised ever higher the quality and standards we now enjoy.

By 1963 the leagues were reaching the stage of being funnelled down into a more rational setup, channelling into the North Staffs and South Cheshire League where the best traditions of good governance and ever improving playing and umpiring standards would come together.

Cricket locally however still presented a vastly different picture fifty years ago than it does today. Still within living memory are the quaint experiences which went along with being a spectator of local cricket in the sixties. Primitive toilet arrangements (remember one 'olers and two'olers?); boys putting up the scores with tins; collecting buckets being passed around for any player who notched a fifty or took five wickets; wooden benches full of splinters; tea served in proper cups; the crucial nearby telephone box from where the latest scoreboard would be sent to the Sentinel which faithfully printed every up to date detail of each game, in all divisions, and followed it up with a stop-press score. Newspapers can no longer provide such a service but the Sentinel thankfully continues to give full support to the league.

The League's cricket arenas would now be unrecognisable to those who watched cricket half a century ago. Millions of pounds have been expended on all the features which make watching the game a more welcoming experience. Brick pavilions with toilets and running water are perhaps the most revolutionary transformation from the past, followed by the vast improvements in ground conditions. Wickets are now infinitely better prepared, sight screens put in place, comfortable seats installed. All this thanks to generous grants from various government and local bodies and, vitally, to the unstinting labour of countless volunteers – the ordinary supporters. They are the greatest asset of all without them the clubs would not survive.

The game moves on apace – thankfully some things remain. Cheerfully packing the cricket bag, with never failing anticipation of the game ahead; the flying catch in the slips, the arcing ball trimming the bails, the cover drive skimming over the turf; the after game conviviality; then the coming out onto the ground as the light leaves the sky, to the lonely call of the owl in his chapel in the oak and the swooping pigeon late home.

This is the stuff of dreams, kept safe in our beautiful game.

Fifty years on and counting......

BREAKAWAY CLUBS TO OPERATE
NEW LEAGUE IN 1963 SEASON

Extracts (1963) reproduced courtesy of the Sentinel

The severance of the Senior "A" clubs from North Staffordshire and District Cricket League now seems to be complete and they will play this season as their new organisation, the North Staffordshire and South Cheshire League, which was formed some weeks ago.

Last night the Senior "A" teams met and decided to go their own way after the rejection of their offer by Senior "B" clubs for a status quo this season, and negotiations between the two sides.

Mr J. E. V. Toney of Stone, Chairman of the new league, said that the 12 Senior "A" clubs were in entire agreement with the steps taken.

When he heard of the decision Mr. Arthur Hodson, President of the North Staffordshire and District League, had this to say:-

"Senior "A" have sacrificed membership of the second oldest cricket league in the country to improve the quality of their cricket. I applaud their courage, but doubt their wisdom.

Unfortunately, in acting as they have, they have jeopardised the ambitions of Senior "B" clubs to play in a higher class of cricket. However, the game is greater than the clubs and I hope both groups will give us good cricket during 1963. I wish them well.

In the meantime I suggest the formation of a joint co-ordinating committee so that shall get co-operation and not competition, and pave the way towards reunion."

"TRAGEDY"

Mr. P. Coxon, a spokesman for Senior "B" clubs, made these comments:-

"It is most regrettable. The tragedy is that at no time have the two sides got together to sort out their differences. Had they done so they would have been able to dispel some of the mistrust which seems to be there.

I am sure that the vast majority of the people concerned in this dispute sincerely want the North Staffordshire and District League to retain the present membership, but it looks as though they are going to be disappointed."

The situation was considered at the monthly meeting of the North Staffordshire and District Cricket League the following week when the resignations by Senior "A" clubs were accepted with regret.

SENIOR "A" EXPLAINS ITS CASE: STATEMENT FROM J.E.V. TONEY, CHAIRMAN OF NORTH STAFFORDSHIRE AND SOUTH CHESHIRE CRICKET LEAGUE.

As so much ill-informed comment has appeared in the Press, which to say the least has not contributed to a solution of a difficult problem, we feel that a final statement of the Senior "A" clubs position is necessary.

After the last Annual Meeting of the North Staffs and District Cricket League, the Chairmen of the Senior "A" Clubs met to consider the position of the Senior Clubs of the League and the completely negative position they held with 12 votes to Senior "A" Clubs and 16 to the other Clubs, with a two-thirds majority required to alter anything and the obvious great difficulty this presented in getting anything wanted by the Senior Clubs changed.

They decided to try and correct this, for them, a difficult and unjust situation within the framework of the present League, by constitutional means.

They asked for a Special General Meeting of the League to be called as provided for in the rules and notified four requests they considered necessary and desirable to be considered. The League meeting took place and their requests were turned down.

They then reluctantly started to consider the formation of a new League in which they would be able to control their own affairs. This was subsequently done.

They then received a proposal from Senior "B" members of the League, the only one received. This in no way met any of their requirements and, in fact, suggested the alteration of the Senior "A" section (to 14 Clubs) to suit the Senior "B" members. This was obviously completely unacceptable to the Senior Clubs as was the suggestion referred to in the February 21st issue of the Sentinel, which did not come from Senior "A" Clubs and had never even been discussed by them.

In their desire to remain in the North Staffordshire and District League, which they had over the years contributed so much to, they decided, however, to make a final attempt for unity and withdrew three-quarters of their requests, stating they were prepared to play in the North Staffordshire and District League in 1963, thereby giving time for negotiation to take place with the only provision that a status quo should operate for 1963 only – surely under the circumstances a most generous gesture.   This was turned down by the Senior "B" Clubs.

No one regrets more than Senior "A" members themselves the necessity for them to leave the League of which they have been members for so long.

SENIOR "B" VIEW: EXTEND THE LEAGUE:
PROMOTION, RELEGATION "LIFEBLOOD"

Though the breakaway of the Senior "A" Clubs now seemed to be final, it should not be regarded as a mortal blow, said Mr.Harry Brough, proposing a toast to the North Staffordshire and District Cricket League at the Silverdale CC Annual Dinner Dance at Longton on Saturday.

Mr. Brough thought new horizons had been opened up. There was no reason why the League should not be extended with promotion and relegation – "the lifeblood of the League" – retained.
Silverdale, one of the founder members, were very proud of their association with the League and thought it sad that they had been deserted by some very old friends. He hoped the breakaway Clubs would find their cricket just as enjoyable in their "greener pastures"

Saying he had encountered a growing hostility everywhere to the breakaway, Mr.Brough added "I believe that if we belong to an ordered society, we have to accept the laws that society imposes upon us. It is a pity the laws of the League were not accepted and the matter settled in the normal way. Cricket is a game, not a big business, however, Senior "B" Clubs can be counted on to guarantee the future of the League"

Mr.Peter Coxon, Assistant League Secretary, who responded, said the surprising thing about the dispute was that the majority of people involved did not want the breakaway. What had gone wrong was that the two sides had never met to thrash the matter out. The spokesmen for both sides were very sincere men, who believed they had done their best to preserve the League. Both sides thought they had bent over backwards to make concessions. He added: "We got so near. It is a tragedy we did not go just that bit further. The future is bright, however, and we look to Clubs like Silverdale to lend support and experience to the second oldest League in the Country".

Mr. Arthur Hodson, League President, in a toast to the Club said "In more than 70 years you have built up a tradition of loyalty to the League setting an example some of our more prosperous Clubs would do well to copy. More prosperity does not necessarily mean more Club spirit or more people who are interested in keeping alive the traditions of the Club and of cricket generally"

PROSPECTS FOR NEW CRICKET LEAGUE

"The North Staffordshire and South Cheshire Cricket League start their first season on Saturday.

Composed of last season's North Staffordshire and District Senior "A" Clubs, the new League will be all out to show the public that their breakaway was for the good of the game.

Here are prospects for the new season:-

Bignall End:
With John Ikin, the former Lancashire and England all-rounder, continuing as Captain, Bignall End has no need of a professional. Veteran N. Roberts assisted by M. Perkins should help to supply the majority of the runs along with L. Riley and F. Shufflebotham. P. Howell now claims a regular first team place and should share the bowling successes with Arthur Burgess, who has now become Secretary. Another veteran, George Lawton will again keep wicket and K. Dutton has returned from Great Chell.

Crewe L.M.R:
The 1961 and 1962 champions will again have as their Captain and Professional, the brilliant all-rounder D.F. Cox who is under contract for 1963 and 1964. Other regulars to support him in the batting are G. Hardstaff, G. Clarke, B. Huff and M. Towneley, with bowing support from R. Vickers and Crewe Footballer, Eric Barnes. Crewe has adequate reserve strength having won everything they attempted in 1962.

Great Chell:
Trevor Goddard's successor as Professional is Indian Test player Salim Durani. He is a left-hand bat and left-arm spinner who has played for Stockport in the Central Lancashire League. John Bailey, who has been Great Chell's wicket keeper for some years, succeeds N.D. Morley as Captain. Newcomers are batsmen H. Cartlidge from Stoke MO and M. Haydon from Knypersley. The bowling support should come from T. Bryan, D. Billings and D. Moorcroft.

Knypersley:
The position of B. Jackson, the Knypersley fast bowler professional, is a little obscure, as he may be required by Derbyshire. J. Bailey, former Staffordshire wicketkeeper, will captain the side, whose batting will come from I. Frost, opening bat and County wicketkeeper, B. Sherratt, B. Street and J. Oakes, Bowling support for Jackson – if he is available, will again come from W. Boon, F. Ryles and K. Young (the only bowler to perform a hat trick in last year's Senior "A".)

Leek:
Lancashire all-rounder, R. Collins is the Professional for 1963 and is noted for big hitting. The dour J. Burton, whose Captaincy and batting have been invaluable to his side in the last two seasons, loses the Captaincy to veteran C. Bonsall, who emerges from retirement. M. Goddard has returned from Norton and should strengthen the batting. Adequate bowling support should come from veteran F.T. Boulton and S. Trafford.

Longton:
L.H.R. Ralph, the former Essex all-rounder continues as Professional and coach. Captain D. Henson will have a good all-round side to manage with batsmen of the calibre of F. Colclough and T.L. Whittaker and bowling support from K. Gallimore and R. de Ville, who plays for Derbyshire II. B. Rowse returns from Army service, during which he scored a century for the Army in Kenya against a South African select XI and J. Allerton, medium-fast bowler, moves over from Sneyd.

Nantwich:
Veteran Geoff Bull has played 27 years without missing a match with Nantwich – an incredible record not only of keenness, but of fitness. He now feels that a younger man should take over the Captaincy when the appointment is made. Nantwich still hope to purchase their own ground and are working towards that end. R. Robbins, who plays for Cheshire, K. Srinivasan (who has played senior cricket in India) and B. Shreeve should get plenty of runs, with the new Professional, Ian Glover, an Australian who played as an amateur with Stockport in 1962. G. Clayton and R. Sherratt supplying bowling.

Newcastle & Hartshill:
As champions of the Senior "B" Section of the North Staffordshire and District League for 1962, Newcastle & Hartshill now venture into higher – class cricket. Two men who helped their rise, professional D. Steele and amateur S. Crump will be missing. Steele having joined Northamptonshire and Crump having transferred to Kidsgrove. They must, therefore, rely heavily on their new professional from Ceylon, Bob Bartels, who is an experienced professional in the Lancashire League and A.W. Morley, who will have a heavy responsibility as both Captain and opening batsman.

Norton:
Veteran professional C. G. Pepper, an Australian with years of League experience in Lancashire, will complete his two years contract with Norton prior to the arrival of G. Sobers in 1964. J. Flannery, the Captain, B. Newton, D. Bean and P. Gibbs should supply the runs, Gibbs having played for the English Schools XI in 1968. The bowling strength is not so obvious, with D. Wilson not having such a good support.

Porthill Park:
There are very few changes at Porthill where D. Whiston an aggressive batsman, is again Captain and the evergreen S. Norcup is professional once more. County player D.A. Hancock, D. Hughes, G. Morrey and J. Moore are all good batsmen. The bowling does not appear strong enough to challenge for honours and F. Taylor has yet to make his "debut" which was prevented by injury in 1962.

Sneyd:
Captain J. Hall gave the team confidence in themselves in 1962 andfinally welded a side capable of the highest quality of cricket. Sneyd have no professional, but will arouse everyone's admiration if J. Hall, A. Rogerson, B. Coates and A. Harrison repeat the splendid batting performance in the latter half of 1962. The bowling needs strength with the loss of J. Allerton to Longton, but David Steele's brother, J. Steele might well prove a match winner.

Stone:
The professional, F. Butler will again Captain the side as evidence of his all round ability in club and county cricket over the years. Stone were not too impressive as a run-getting side last year, but the normal form of R. Tobias, P. Shardlow, K. Ahmad and M. Middleton should remedy this deficiency. D. Babb, second in the averages for 1962 and J. Harvey are two bowlers who could help Stone to challenge for the leadership.

THE FIRST 50 YEARS by Stuart Williamson

When I was asked to write a foreword to the Book by the 50th Anniversary Celebration Committee, I did wonder if I would be suitably qualified. Would I be able to provide any extra that would compliment the first 50 years of our Cricket League, the players, professionals or amateurs, the administrators and spectators, grounds men/Umpires and not least, the ladies who have been involved over this period of time, here are my thoughts.

I joined Porthill Park Cricket Club in 1974, 11 years after the formation of the League in 1963, so I missed the halcyon days of the revered Professionals such as Sobers, Hall and Gilchrist plus many others and the many tales of deeds done on the cricket field. However, the authors of the book have been able to capture some of these moments and the whole history of the League.

What has struck me whilst I have been playing and involved in administration, is the number of changes that have taken place over the first fifty years of the League.

Perhaps the first milestone was in the early 1980's when Stafford and Little Stoke joined the League followed swiftly by ten further Clubs.

This was followed in the late 1990's and early 2000's with the ECB creating Premier Leagues up and down the Country to provide a link between the Amateur and Professional games. This brought substantial funding for the League and also considerable administration for the League and the Clubs.

Just as the Premier League was commencing two other major factors influenced our local cricket, the National Lottery/Sport England and Sky being awarded the broadcasting rights; like our other game Football, this brought huge changes to our League and I don't think there is one Club who has not had a grant, loan or Lottery award.

The development of facilities for cricketers and members has truly been phenomenal. You only have to look at Clubs in this area who have accessed these funds which has led to new Pavilions, Nets, Sight Screens and Electric Scoreboards – a welcome boost to the area.

The other major transformation in the early 2000's was, of course, the merger with the North Staffs and District Cricket League which brought the two Leagues together and created the promotion and relegation structure which we have today. The League coming full circle from our early beginnings.

There are, of course, many other aspects of change during this first 50 years i.e., T20, Coloured clothing, Websites, Computer Scoring, Live Scores, Development Sides, Club Mark. All of these are evolving and to its credit, this has kept our League at the forefront of recreational Cricket nationally. We are as strong as ever and recently our League side have won the President's Cup five years in succession.

All of the above would not have happened without the assistance of the League Manager, Keith Tunnicliffe, and present and past members of the Executive, Management Committee, Umpires and Sponsors , which have enabled this League to grow and flourish.

Hopefully their efforts have enabled countless players, volunteers and spectators to enjoy week-end Cricket in the area. Well done to you all.

I must also make one further thank you to the 50th Anniversary Celebration Committee for all their hard work in making this record of our first 50 years. My special thanks go to Tony Loffill, Derek Rowley, Jim Rowley and Brian Lawton for all their hard work in making this publication possible.

I hope you have as much pleasure as I have in reading the book and having a permanent record of our first 50 years.

I hope the next 50 years are as good as the first.

Launch of the Exhibition for the 50th Anniversary with League officials and Sponsors.

NORTH STAFFORDSHIRE & SOUTH CHESHIRE
PREMIER CRICKET LEAGUE CLUBS
FOUNDER MEMBER CLUBS - 1963
Former Senior "A" of the North Staffordshire and District Cricket League (Est 1889)

BIGNALL END	NANTWICH (to 1995)
CREWE	NEWCASTLE & HARTSHILL (to 2001)
GREAT CHELL (to 1989)	NORTON
KNYPERSLEY	PORTHILL PARK
LEEK	SNEYD (to 2003)
LONGTON	STONE

ADDITIONAL CLUBS ON EXPANSION/PROMOTION

1979
LITTLE STOKE
STAFFORD
1980
BARLASTON
BETLEY
BURSLEM
BUXTON (to 2000)
CAVERSWALL
CHEADLE
CREWE ROLLS-ROYCE (to 1999)
ELWORTH
KIDSGROVE
LEYCETT
1983
ASHCOMBE PARK (to 2000)
AUDLEY
1989
MODDERSHALL
1996
CHECKLEY
HASLINGTON (to 2006)
MEIR HEATH
2001
NORTON IN HALES (to 2004)
2002
RODE PARK & LAWTON
2004
HEM HEATH
2005
WOOD LANE
2006
ASHCOMBE PARK
BAGNALL
BLYTHE
BUXTON

CREDA/STANFIELDS (to 2009)
ECCLESHALL
ENDON
FENTON
HANFORD (to 2007)
J & G MEAKIN
NEWCASTLE & HARTSHILL
NORTON-IN-HALES
OAKAMOOR
OULTON
SANDYFORD
SILVERDALE
SWYNNERTON PARK
WEDGWOOD
WESTON
WHITMORE
WOORE
2007
MODDERSHALL "A" (to 2012)
2008
ALSAGER
PORTHILL PARK "A" (to 2010)
FORSBROOK (to 2009)
2009
HANFORD
2010
WOOTTON (to 2011)
2011
NORTON IN HALES (to 2013)
2012
CHURCH EATON
2013
LEEK MOORLANDS
2014
MODDERSHALL "A"

ALSAGER CC

The first records of Alsager Cricket Club date back to 1874 when Alsager beat Kidsgrove CC by an innings. The club was later reformed (in 1882) by the rector George Skene who represented Eton at cricket and rowing as well as being a champion boxer and a chess master The club moved to the Parsonage Field in 1904, by now playing in the North Staffordshire Combination League.

The First World War brought cricket to a halt and only in 1930 was a committee formed by Charlie Bourne to re-establish the club. Games were again played on the Parsonage Field.

By the 1950's the club were settled in their ground with a thriving membership and with two teams playing at week-ends. In 1953 the council purchased the land from the church and asked the club to find a new home. Donations were sought from members and the club purchased two fields, incorporating an orchard, an open ditch and a number of very large trees. The trees had to be removed with dynamite and the wet land was drained at great expense by members such as Charlie Bennion, Len Cliff, Harry Hancock, Joe Edwards, Joe Bebbington and Bill Rawlings. The final cost of the work was £11000

In 1955 Alsager assisted in the formation of the Cheshire County Cricket Conference and in 1956 played their first match at the Fairview Ground where a new pavilion was built in 1957.

In 1971 the club re-entered the Kidsgrove Junior League after being a founder member and celebrated in 1974 when the Colts won the cup.

The club's first major success came in 1972 when it won the Pennant Trophy with players such as Nigel Lobley, Derek Pointon, Chris Timewell, Richard Henshall and Kevin Birks.

Alsager's square was always challenging with scores above 150 relatively rare. In 1973 Bert Flack, the Lancashire and England groundsman was engaged to formulate a plan to make necessary improvements.

The senior sides were by now playing in the more competitive Cheshire League and stalwarts like Eddie Gilhooley, Steve Armitage and Richard Bason were making their debuts. Gilhooley was captain when the Cheshire League Championship was won in 1992 with a huge input from the influential Mike Tudor and ex-Stoke goalkeeper Ken South.

In 1993 Alsager joined the expanding Cheshire County League and in 1994 finished in runners up position. They also won the League Cup in 1995 and 1997 with tremendous match winning contributions from Chris Welch whose father Eric played as a professional in North Staffordshire for many years.

In 2008 the club unanimously decided to join the North Staffs and South Cheshire League and entered in the Third Division. The club engaged the services of Shaun Rashid as their first professional and under the captaincy of Alan Stancliffe and with a plethora of runs from Paul Pickford, Paul Tibbetts and Mohammed Arshad won the Division at the first attempt.

The club remained in Division Two until 2012 when club captain Oliver Sadler guided the club into Division One after some high quality contributions from Gareth Rowe, Paul Newnes and Sean Price.

In 2013 the club's U17s again won its section in the Kidsgrove League and with the U11s and the U13s winning their respective leagues the future continues to look bright.

Finally, at the beginning of 2013 the club received an Olympic Legacy grant which enabled major refurbishment to take place, allowing the club to continue to make the sound progress which will secure the future of this much travelled club for years to come.

ASHCOMBE PARK CC

Ashcombe Park are thought to have begun life in 1865, settling in the 1870's in the grounds of the Ashcombe Park Estate.

A remarkable match on the ground in 1882 saw the Ashcombe professional, James Walker, take nine wickets, eight in successive deliveries, without conceding a run, dismissing visitors Tunstall for just two runs.

The club was a founder member of the Churnet Valley League before joining the North Staffs and District League soon after the First World War. A legendary bowler in the 1920's was Obadiah Brassington.

Ashcombe Park entered a golden period in the late 1950's with a team that included Fred Taylor, Khurshid "Charlie" Ahmed who had come to England with the first Pakistan touring team and – as professional – Sonny Ramadhin, the legendary West Indian spin bowler. Promotion to the "A" Division was followed by successive League Championship titles in 1959 and 1960 when Ramadhin took over a hundred wickets in each season. The club has always vigorously denied the claims made by losing teams that the wickets were specially prepared for the spinning wizard. He was playing at Ashcombe Park in 1959 when Norton were the visitors, captained by Frank Worrell, the future West Indian skipper. Press reports estimated a crowd of over three thousand turning up to watch the game.

Ashcombe remained in the District League in the sixties, winning the championship again in 1966. Eventually the club opted to apply for membership of the growing North Staffs and South Cheshire League and was duly elected for the 1984 season.

Former Northamptonshire all rounder Brian Crump became Ashcombe professional for three seasons before Ian Wilson took the captaincy in 1988 and with Ross Salmon, who had risen through Ashcombe's junior ranks to become club professional, another successful period began. Salmon scored well over ten thousand runs during his eleven seasons as professional and formed a formidable alliance with fellow opening bat Phil Hawkins. For many years the pair held the record for the biggest opening partnership in both Division One and Division Two of the NSSCL. Terry Eyre became the leading wicket taker for the club in the NSSCL era until he was recently overtaken by David Clowes.

Ashcombe won promotion to the top division in 1990 and was runner up for the title in 1991 before winning the NSSC League Championship in 1992. A period of decline at the turn of the century has been reversed with Ashcombe steadily on the rise again, winning promotion to the Division One of the now expanded league in 2012.

Like many clubs Ashcombe Park has always had strong family connections with succeeding generations appearing for the club. Very few seasons in living memory have gone by at Ashcombe without the names of Alcock, Pegg, Profitt or Goodwin featuring in one of the elevens.

The club enjoys a magnificent setting with outstanding views of the Staffordshire Moorlands; and in recent years the committee has overseen construction of a new dressing room and scorebox together with a major extension to and refurbishment of what is now a splendid clubhouse, enabling Ashcombe Park to become the focal point for much of the social life in and around Cheddleton.

AUDLEY CC

Adley, Madeley, Keele and 'Castle
Uxton, Mucc'stone. 'Ale n'Assel

As the old rhyme shows, Audley has long featured in the history of the county since its Lords occupied the ancient keep of Heighley Castle. Their descendants were certainly playing at bat and ball in the mid nineteenth century. A game took place against Rode Park in 1745 on the old Mill Field ground. This was the club's home until a move was made to the present site, Kent Hills, in 1885. Not many clubs can claim to have played their cricket in the same venue for so long. Over the years gradual improvements and additions have been effected, with major changes in the 1920's when a new pavilion and scorebox were built. With a grant from the Lord's Taverners a new pavilion was erected in 1963, followed two years later by a new scorebox, dedicated to the memory of Joseph Glover who supported the club through his lifetime.

The club lived on a diet of friendly cricket until becoming members of the North Staffs League and maintained its membership after the Great War in what had become the North Staffs and District League. The Second World War brought another interruption to league activity, but Audley welcomed peacetime cricket by winning the Senior "B" Championship in 1946 – only to find that there was to be no promotion that year!. A series of good years followed this success. In 1963 Audley finally gained promotion to the Senior "A" competition and carried off the Championship three times in 1964, 1971 and 1982. In 1983 the club moved into Division One B of the North Staffs and South Cheshire League. – This after a short period of confusion when it seemed that with Ashcombe Park the club might not have a league to play in. It was even suggested that the two clubs might have to meet week by week for the season 22 times in all. The bluff was happily called and the League found the club a home after all.

Audley has always been the model of a close knit community and generations of the same families have represented the village. Platt, Leek, Wareham, Shuker, Ratcliffe and Fryer are just a selection of the well known names to which can be added one of the local legends, Fred Bailey, a highly talented batsman who played for his county on many occasions and who left the club for various locations before returning to play his final playing years for his old club. Arthur Broadbent was another who is remembered, in particular for the feat of taking two hat tricks in one eight ball over.

Cricket of some sort carried on throughout the war years, largely because there would be a supply of men in reserved occupation. Two names that have come to be of interest to followers of football would be those of Frankie Soo, a Stoke City wing half of Oriental extraction (Did he bowl Chinamen? will be understood only by those of a certain age); and of Denis Herod, a fine footballer who was Stoke City's regular goalkeeper in the 40's and 50's.

Harry Hancock was the first of the club's professionals, signed in 1953 and he was succeeded by another Audley immortal Vic Burgess, described by the Audley historian as a "superb bowler who could move the ball both ways". He spent nine years as professional with the remarkable record of 757 wickets at a cost of 7.8 runs each. Then came Terry Harrison "the Windmill"; and then, from another iconic cricketing family, Northants all rounder Brian Crump.

Mention should here be made of the historian. Philip ("Horace") Emberton was an archetypical one club man, one of the products of the now disappeared Wolstanton Grammar School who made a significant impact in local club cricket in the fifties and sixties. A wicket keeper, he played for the club for many years.

For the first seasons in the North Staffs and South Cheshire League Mark Davies took over the role as professional. His Shropshire roots and his outstanding ability took him to the captaincy of his county. Then John Potts took over and stayed for four years. On his watch in 1987 the club won Division One B and the Talbot Cup.

Alan Griffiths came to the club in 1987. He was the regular Staffordshire wicket keeper, immediately appointed club captain and was undoubtedly the most successful skipper in Audley's history. Honours flowed when he was with the club: two championships, three Talbot Cups and one Staffs Cup as well as being named seven times the league's most sporting club.

Since there has been a litany of highly achieving professionals: Barrington Browne, the most feared paceman in the league who took 243 wickets in three seasons; then mystery spinner Aamer Wasim, also responsible for hatfuls of victims. T.P Singh was a memorable all rounder from India. Alfonso Thomas, the South African all rounder now on the books of Somerset, was club professional in 2006 and 2007 when Audley won a third title.

Over the years Audley has been known for positive cricket, sportsmanship, wonderful teas and an excellent social life. Each club has its fair share of characters and Audley is no exception with the likes of its late groundsman John Hinks and its band of loyal supporters. With clubs like Audley on the scene the league will continue to thrive.

BAGNALL CC

This tranquil village was first recorded in the Doomsday Book but it was some years later that the village headmaster, Mr D.K.Gibbs who launched the idea of a cricket club in Bagnall. A meeting was called at the 16th Century Stafford Arms in the village on September 3rd 1951 and a committee duly chosen. No time was lost in finding a playing pitch. Mr J.C.Lord was approached and he gave permission for the club to use a field in Light Oaks which was subsequently purchased.

The first club captain was Alan Capey and a typical early fixture was the one against the PMT (younger cricketers will need an explanation: it has nothing to do with a physical condition of the same name.). Unfortunately details of Bagnall's early years are scarce; but it is known that Mr Gibbs was the first Bagnall player to score a hundred. His son Peter, later of Derbyshire, played his first cricket at Bagnall. Remarkably for a small club Bagnall has produced two first class players. Andrew Brassington, son of one of the founder members, went on to have a successful career as Gloucester's wicket keeper.

After some years in the South Cheshire Alliance, Bagnall in 2006 joined the North Staffs and South Cheshire League. The club celebrated its 60th anniversary with a double triumph. The First XI won the Division Three title while the Second XI also gained promotion as runners up in Division 3B. The club has also been expert in choosing its professionals. In 2012 Asif Raza took 104 wickets, a record in Division 3; while in 2013 Asif Ahmad Khan achieved a ten wicket haul against Weston.

Andrew Bramhall was the club scorer in the 1960's when his father Neville was wicket keeper. His father, now age 87, lives in Stone, and recalls with pleasure his happy times at the club. These are a few of his memories:

"Some of the names I remember from my days at the club are Ken Evans, Wilf and Patrick Hancock, Eric Holdcroft and Derek Worthy, (whose name occurs elsewhere in these pages) who later became secretary of the South Cheshire Alliance. I was the Secretary of the Ceramic Research in Penkhull and had a long career in junior school cricket. I joined Bagnall in 1960 after playing in other places. I batted against Brian Statham whose bowling kept passing me like a tuning fork.

When I first played at Bagnall the only accommodation was the body of a van on the lower side of the ground by Ken Evan's wall and access to the ground was by the lane to his frontage. We bought the pavilion for £50 from the NCB cricket ground off Victoria Road in Fenton, transported it to Bagnall and erected it ourselves. Derek Worthy and I dug a sewer connection about 100 yards long to the sewers in Ken Evans' lane and installed a toilet at the back of the pavilion. If we hadn't done that the ladies would never have come to cut the sandwiches. A couple of years later we made the entrance from Bagnall Road.

My best wishes go to the club that was once dear to me."

Golden memories of the wonderful and eccentric days of village cricket at Bagnall.

BARLASTON CC

BARLASTON C.C.
Est.1868

The origins of Barlaston Cricket Club can be traced back to 1868. The centenary was celebrated with games against the Midland Club Conference, the President's Eleven and the Staffordshire Gentlemen. A large marquee hosted cocktail parties to welcome representatives from many clubs in the area.

The first club might have been in the form of a country house team with its centre at Barlaston Hall; in those times the Broughton-Adderleys owned a large estate which included Barlaston village.

At the beginning of the last century an old railway carriage served as the pavilion for the thirty or forty members which constituted the club and matches were played against teams long gone – Bucknall, Basford, Etruria and Wolstanton among them. Funds were raised through dances and whist drives and the total income did not rise above twenty pounds a year. Records are lost of activities during the years of the First World War no records were kept but in 1918 Mrs Broughton- Adderley wrote to the secretary instructing him to remind the farmer that the field was given for cricket and that her three sons serving in France would be most displeased to hear otherwise. In 1956 the ground was finally purchased by the Parish Council and let to the club at a peppercorn rate. The money needed was raised by the wealthy pottery manufacturers who lived in the village.

The twenty years following the purchase of the ground saw the greatest period of Barlaston's development, when playing success earned a place in the North Staffs and South Cheshire League in 1980. In the late 60's the Saturday eleven went through the whole season undefeated while the Sunday eleven took on some of the strongest clubs in the Midlands and suffered only one defeat.

Barlaston has remained essentially a village club. Players and officials have a strong connection with nearby Blurton and in particular with the High School. The five officers in situ have been associated with the club for a total of over two hundred years. Membership is small except for the junior section which over recent years has blossomed into an excellent training facility for local youngsters many of whom have represented the district and the county.

Barlaston is blessed with its picturesque ground. The committee roll up their sleeves and take good care of the square. They are the successors of "Fred" Chollerton, groundsman and general factotum of the club during the fifties and the sixties. Fred, a master craftsman at Wedgwood produced a pint mug on which was painted the names of Barlaston's opponents. It was called "The

Captain's pot" and was kept at The Duke of York for the opposition captain to use.

Barlaston has enjoyed many successes in their time in the league with room to develop further as a Premier league club. The support that the club enjoys (and which showed itself in the construction of the pavilion) has played a major part in building up The Cricket Field into a wonderful village amenity. Long may it continue.

BETLEY CC

Betley Cricket Club, complete with rules and regulations, was officially formed in 1847. The Staffordshire Advertiser of July 1847 duly recorded a match played by the newly formed club although cricket had been undoubtedly played in the village long before.

The Gentlemen of Etruria came to Betley that July. (Was there a 'Wedgwood' name in the eleven?) The report of this early Victorian match presents a charming window into village cricket in the long ago. "The early part of the day was very unfavourable for the game: nevertheless the wickets were pitched at around about 12 o'clock and very shortly after the weather turned out as fine as the most ardent lover of the game could wish". As each club had been established about the same length of time and this was the first challenge the Betley club had accepted since its formation the result was awaited with great interest and anxiety. The fielding of the Etruria club was admired, as was the bowling of the Betley club. Betley was successful with 10 wickets to spare, Etruria having obtained 44 runs in two innings and Betley 45.

Where precisely this match was played is not known. A game played in 1860 is more informative about the venue. This was an encounter with Muckleston in the grounds of Betley Hall "in the presence of a large and fashionable company."

Games like these quoted would count as events of huge significance in nineteenth century village life. The cricket club was a social as well as a sporting club and the came to represent the village. Oral records suggest that there may have been two teams playing in Betley in the grounds of the Court and the Hall; and another team playing in neighbouring Wrinehill. These were all friendly fixtures (on paper at least) encompassing teams like the Nantwich Mechanics Institute, Muckleston, Crewe, Audley, Silverdale, Doddington, Madeley and Lawton Hall

It was not until 1904 that Betley began to play league cricket by joining the North Staffs and District Combination District One. In 1920 the club joined the newly formed Section B of the North Staffs and District League.

The club moved to its present ground in 1946 when a huge amount of work was carried out by members in the construction of a square. The outfield remained the domain of the grazing cattle belonging to Betley Court. Progress of a sort was achieved in 1951 when the club's landlord and president, captain Fletcher-Twemlow gave permission for the tall rough grass which covered the out field to be cut twice per season.

The club continued to prosper. In 1980 it joined the North Staffs and South Cheshire League. Two years later its most famous son, Dominic Cork, made his debut at the age of eleven. By the age of twenty he was club professional before leaving to join Derbyshire on the road to a spectacular career. He maintained his links with the club where, famously, his mother was responsible for the teas. His deeds are recorded more fully elsewhere in this publication.

Betley: the archetypical English village club, representing all that is best in the game.

BIGNALL END CC

1875

Cricket in the North owes an immense debt to coalpits and Methodism. The mines and the chapels brought communities together in unique fashion and cricket was a vital part in the social scene. So it was with Bignall End, caught in history at Tibbs Craft in 1875, whence it moved in 1887 to Boon Hill, its present site. The club's cricket prospered and in 1890 it joined the newly formed North Staffs and District League.

The club did experience hard times. Many of its players had lost their lives in the great local mining disaster of 1895 and the club experienced some lean years, slipping in and out of the league twice before the advent of the Great War.

The war years brought the suspension of the league and Bignall End joined the long forgotten War Workers League where the club enjoyed a great deal of success for which the players obviously developed a liking. In 1923, 1924, and 1925 the club won the championship of the North Staffs and District League and set a standard which subsequent teams were jealous to protect. Between the wars there was a steady stream of quality players representing the club, most of them from local families. The Burgesses come to mind whose feats are still recalled in village folklore. Bowling out Meakins for six runs demands a second look in any club history; while both achieved the feat of taking "all ten". In 1949 Arthur dismissed 10 Knypersley batsmen for 31, a performance which must have rankled with his brother Vic who in 1953 saw off ten men of Stone for 23. The twins had sound support from the Ikins, the Mayers and the Locketts, all representatives of celebrated local families

Many players made a name for themselves in local cricket while others progressed to wider horizons. Geoff Goodwin moved to represent Leicestershire, Aaron Lockett pursued a successful career in the Birmingham and Lancashire Leagues. (His story is told elsewhere in this book,) John Ikin and Bob Taylor both England Test players, belonged to the Bignall End club.

In nineteen sixty three came the parting of the ways when twelve clubs took the decision to form the North Staffs and South Cheshire League. A decision had to be made. Leave the North Staffs and District? After much heart searching it was decided that since the new league offered the likelihood of a higher standard of cricket it would be in the clubs interest to throw in its lot with the NSSCL.

The 60's and 70's rewarded this decision with periods of relative success. The 80's brought a decline in fortunes however and the club slid down the divisions. But a club with almost one hundred and fifty years of history has by no means lost heart. Bad years have been replaced by good ones and the club is determined to rise again from its current lowly position to play again in the top reaches of local cricket.

Cricket in North Staffordshire and South Cheshire has written a wonderful story and Bignall End is proud to have contributed to it.

BLURTON / HEM HEATH / FORSBROOK CC

The club was formed in 1948 and until the mid eighties teachers made up the bulk of the team which played its matches on school grounds in Blurton. The Council's care was very desultory – rain would mean no grass cutting with the result that some of the games were played on an outfield ankle deep. A team amassing a hundred runs in its innings on those pitches was unlikely to lose the game. Nonetheless they were good days, leaving many happy memories in their wake.

Players changed and took tea in the school cloakrooms which were also the base for our scorer, the legendary Mrs Storey, whose sons and grandsons took over the duties on her retirement.

In the mid eighties Blurton went through a time where its future was in doubt as players retired or moved to clubs with better facilities. Many went to Wedgwoods whose ground was the best in the Stone League and far superior to anything the Blurton club could offer. Nonetheless the club survived and grew stronger again as a team. What was still lacking though was a clubhouse which assured the nearby Marsden pub pints and quarts of good business.

After twice winning the Stone League Premier title the club applied to join the North Staffs District League only to be turned down because of the ground. This meant approaching local farmers as the search went on for a suitable site, culminating in eventual success which was to presage a new and exciting era.

Two years and an enormous amount of hard work around 1990 – when the club again won the Stone League title – saw Blurton finally accepted into the North Staffs and District League. The name was changed in 1993 to Forsbrook, where the new ground was sited. Promotion was achieved in 1995 to the dizzy heights of Senior "A", a level that proved too exalted in the event, leading to relegation after only one season.

For financial reasons the decision was taken to move back to the Stone League, where Blurton took the title in a memorable season.

In 2008 Hem Heath made an approach with a view to a merger. An abundance of youngsters meant a shortage of space and since Forsbrook was suffering from a lack of players it was decided to accept the proposal: a move not universally popular but which guaranteed Blurton's survival at the top level.

Blurton/Forsbrook has been in existence now for 65 years and thanks to the merger with Hem Heath have a wonderful future ahead.

BLYTHE CC

Rain stopped play…. an all too familiar occurrence. Cricketers have developed ways of beguiling the time until the game can resume. One is to name teams of famous players with names of actors, or flowers, or trees – or what about beautiful surnames that have featured in the long history of the game? Grace, Noble, Mead, Verity, Rose, Love, Silverwood… you can complete the list yourself; but don't leave out Colin Blythe, the Kent spinner, whose life was cut short in the First World War by someone who knew nothing of cricket. His name is carried by this village club who can lay claim to the title of the most mellifluous names in the land.

Based at Cresswell sports ground between the villages of Cresswell and Draycott, close to the A50, Blythe was formed in 1926 as a cricket facility for workers at the nearby Blythe Colour Works and remained in the ownership of that company and its successors until 1997 when the cricket club members bought the ground with the assistance of a lottery grant and intensive fund raising. The club was offered the sports ground by the former owners Cookson Matthey and was given a twelve month period in which to raise around thirty thousand pounds. The enthusiasm and commitment shown by club members produced the money on time.

In the 1950's the club was served by professionals such as Maqsood Ahmed and "Dusty" Rhodes; but the longest serving was Vince Lindo who played his cricket with the club from 1969 to 1981. Jehan Mubarak and Ranil Dhammika also featured with the club in more recent years.

The club played much of its Saturday cricket in the North Staffs and District League and joined the North Staffordshire and South Cheshire League in the 2006 expansion, being awarded a place in Division 2. The first season proved difficult and relegation was avoided only because Haslington dropped out of the league. However the club's fortunes were completely revived in the following season, when under the captaincy of Peter Finch the club topped the league and won a place in Division One, where it has remained ever since – carrying off the Barney McArdle Trophy in 2008 as a welcome additional prize.

Blythe is a small rural club with a reputation for developing young players. Six junior teams and three women's teams play under the same banner as the four senior sides. Former Blythe juniors Chris Beech and Matt Goodwin have played Minor Counties cricket for Staffordshire.

A small club – But one that makes its mark in the local scene.

BURSLEM CC

History tells us that of the Six Towns, Burslem is the oldest, the Mother Town, the one of the immortal card, overlooked by the angel on the old town hall. Unfortunately the seraph sees no cricket: Burslem Cricket Club is to be found some miles down the Waterloo Road in Cobridge.

How old is Burslem Cricket Club? Sadly, no one really knows. In 1985 a fire destroyed the old pavilion and all the records kept therein; and it is only because Leek told us about a game played there in 1840 (imagine a trip over the roads to the moorland town in those days) that there are any clues extant about the club's history. There is no doubt however that the Burslem club, sited improbably between the tintamarre of the steel works on one side and the quietude of the Little Sisters of the Poor on the other, provided a high and consistent standard of cricket in its classical industrial home: supported it seems by a specially vociferous band of enthusiasts.

One name that has prevailed through Burslem's life has been that of Briscoe. Billy, Don and Roy were three of the family; and it was the last named who took on the task of organising the construction of a new pavilion. Barlaston church was suffering subsidence problems and had been using a temporary building which Roy acquired for us and which was ready for use in the 1987 season. Although it served its purpose adequately its wood construction offered little security and visits from the local thieves were regular events.

In the early 1990's existence was proving precarious. Then the Cobridge regeneration project came into effect; the old ground was in prime position in an area required for redevelopment. It was suddenly time for hectic planning, discussions and subsequent major reconstruction of the former steel works site, which in turn had been the site of the 1985 garden festival.

As a result of all this change the club was relocated on a site a mere four hundred yards from the previous ground; and funds were obtained from the National Lottery for the erection of a pavilion. Meanwhile the playing area was under preparation: this was part of the bargain the club struck when it agreed to move sites.

Thankfully this time the pavilion was a construction of brick and tile, safe from the plague of break-ins of previous years. However Burslem's troubles were not yet all quite behind it. The club played on its new ground in 1996 only a few months after the turf had been laid. This proved to be a year too soon. There was no option but to play, even though the ground had been given insufficient time to settle since by then the bulldozers were hard at work on the old pitch.

The inevitable consequences now concerned drainage problems. It was the club's ill-luck that a faulty drainage system had been put in and the wrong sort of topsoil applied. Much corrective work had to be carried out before the problems became fewer.

Everyone was sorry to leave the Cobridge home that had seen so many cricketing highlights over so many years and which was part of the long history of cricket in the Potteries. So many local cricketers enjoyed their games played against the backcloth of a scene dominated by canal, steel works and views of bottle kilns and pitheads. What must Basil d'Oliviera have made of all this when as a young man, recently settled in England, he played for a Commonwealth team in a match arranged to mark Stoke on Trent's Golden Jubilee celebrations? Some of his teammates that day were Wes Hall, Roy Gilchrist and Sonny Ramadhin, Cec Pepper and Jack Pettiford. "Dolly" made 83; and made his mark in Burslem's long story.

The club has had myriad characters of its own. One who must be mentioned is Ray Durose, a stick of rock with the name of Burslem running through it. His contribution to the club is impossible to overlook. He typifies the lovers of the game who are indispensible to a cricket club.

The club looks forward to many more years of cricket carrying the name of the Potteries' most historic town.

CAVERSWALL CC

The cricket club was founded in 1889 though the game was undoubtedly played in the village for many years before that. The original club patron was William Eli Blowers, the owner of the castle; and he transformed the village field inside the estate into a cricket pitch complete with square and pavilion in 1889, the same year in which the club earned its first mention in the Sentinel.

By the early 1900's the club had joined the Churnet Valley League and some twenty years later it became a member of the North Staffs league, topping the table of Senior "B" in 1920.

In 1933 the Caverswall Castle premises passed from the hands of the Bowers family into the ownership of the Missionary Sisters and Servants of the Holy Ghost and became a convent for novice nuns. The idea of healthy young men playing cricket on the premises was not a welcome one for the Mother Superior and the club, after much unsuccessful petitioning, was obliged to leave the Castle ground in 1946. What the novices thought is not recorded.

Friendly cricket was now played at various venues until in 1948 a piece of ground was obtained at Bolton Gate in Weston Coyney. This was always going to be a temporary move and the committee continued search for a new venue, finally alighting on the club's present home in mid 1951. Six years later the club was admitted to the North Staffs and District league, the first fixture taking place on Easter Saturday 1957.

In 1957 Harold Boon became club professional who proved his worth as Caverswall's longest serving paid player, giving nine years of service. During his days at the club a junior team was entered in the Kidsgrove and District League for the first time; while Peter Timmis emerged as a brilliant young player who was to represent Staffordshire and the Minor Counties on many occasions. He later became professional at Porthill Park and Leek, returning to Caverswall as club captain in 1984. It was four years later that he was tragically killed in a motor accident.

Until 1981 the club played on in the NSD but in 1981 made a successful application to join the NSSCL where it has played ever since. The club won the Staffordshire Cup in 1992 and carried off the championship of the NSSCL in 1991.

The club celebrated its centenary in 1989, holding a dinner at Trentham Gardens, a marvellous occasion with Brian Close, Kim Barnett, Rob Bailey, Philip Bainbridge adding to the three hundred members past and present.

Alan J Gott became chairman in 1969 and remained in office until his death in 2007. The Caverswall ground has been renamed "The Alan Gott Memorial Ground." In recognition of the great contribution that Alan made to Caverswall Cricket Club.

History and sanctity hover round this unique club.

CHEADLE CC

The pits and the church were cradles of the game in the northern shires and Cheadle Cricket Club fits this familiar pattern. The pits are gone now though Pugin's magnificent church still ennobles the town and will have no doubt blessed the beginnings of the game in its parish.

Attlee Road was the site of cricket activity and the club seems to have played all its games there since earliest days. 1923 was the year when the club made the move to its present ground on Tean Road. This proved to be an excellent decision, providing the solid foundations which the club enjoys today, its future constantly secured by the tenacity and enthusiasm of its members who have raised thousands of pounds over the years.

Until 1909 there were two teams playing competitive cricket in Cheadle. Cheadle Town played at the old Bushes ground where a team made up mainly of industrial workers provided a rival eleven. Local derbies were much anticipated and well supported but ceased when the two clubs decided to amalgamate in 1909.

After the war Cheadle entered the North Staffs and District League, Division Two. Success quickly followed with the winning of the Junior B league championship in 1920. Four years later the club acquired the spacious new Tean Road ground. The club seems to have passed through some difficult years thereafter, reduced to one team in the NSDL and a second eleven in the Blythe Bridge League.

The post war years happily brought a revival in the club's fortunes. A team was put together which began to win matches on a regular basis and attract better players. Interest in the club and its activities grew apace, rewarded again in 1951 by the winning of the Junior "B" Section of the North Staffs and District League. The sixties and seventies proved to be two successful decades with the club's first eleven winning the championship no fewer than eleven times with the club's second eleven frequently chipping in to complete a seasonal double,

In 1981 the club opted for a historic move when it accepted an invitation to join the North Staffs and South Cheshire League. Early success ensued with three Talbot Cup triumphs in the first seven seasons and a league championship in 1993. In these years the two Deans played an imposing role. Steven played many memorable innings for his club and his county which he captained. Kevin, no relation, started his career with Cheadle, going on to represent Derbyshire. He was a very fine bowler unlucky not to have been selected for international honours. John Steele, of the famous Staffordshire dynasty, played in 1969. He went on to Leicestershire and finished his playing days with Glamorgan before becoming a first class umpire.

At present the club operates eight teams ranging from the first eleven to the under 11's. There are several qualified coaches at the club's disposal and practice and net sessions take place each week in the summer

From humble beginnings Cheadle Cricket Club has risen to a position of power and relative prosperity in local cricketing circles. The united and determined effort to maintain the fortunes of the club have ensured the respect and admiration of the cricketing fraternity and laid the foundations for an assured future in the League.

CHECKLEY CC

The club was founded in 1860 as Lower Tean Cricket Club: in a traditional rural setting, playing its games against local villages, travelling by horse and cart. In 1909 the present name was adopted

Lt-Col Philips owned the Heybridge estate and leased the present ground for two ears of corn. These feature still in the club badge of today. In 1921 a batting and a bowling cup were presented by the Philips family, a gift matched by the General Manager of the North Staffs Railway who gave a silver cup for the best fielder. For more than eighty years the cups have been regularly presented, with the winners' names faithfully recorded on engraved shields mounted on the plinths. Checkley cherishes its past as it enjoys its present.

In 1966 Checkley gained admission to the Stone and District League and swiftly moved through all the divisions. In 1974 the club was admitted to the North Staffs and District League where after some initial difficult seasons it achieved promotion to the Senior "A". Meanwhile major ground improvements had been undertaken; and by 1985 the levelling of the pitch and the provision of improved kitchens and toilets with new changing rooms and showers were complete.

In the winter of 1987-88 Checkley made the crucial decision to engage a club professional. One of the first was Paul Taylor who topped the Senior "A" bowling averages in both 1989 and 1990 taking 92 and 106 wickets respectively, Paul went on to represent England (owing a great deal to his sojourn at Checkley, the locals would claim); and then Russell Spiers who followed him with four successful years

In 1996 Checkley had applied for membership of the expanding North Staffordshire and South Cheshire League and were duly admitted to Division Two. After a few quiet seasons promotion was secured to the Senior League in the last match of the campaign. The club by then had Kim Barnett as its professional and he stayed until 2005. He was replaced by Gulam Bodi, a South African, who could not help prevent the club's relegation at the end of the season. In 2008 the club was relegated again as a result of points' deduction. The following year Checkley appointed Andy Carr as captain, stabilising their position in Division Two.

Then in 2009 Checkley, still in Division Two, won the Talbot Cup. In a magnificent final, played at Checkley, Stone's professional, Qaiser Abbas, hit a superb 108 out of an imposing total of 232 in 45 overs, only to be trumped by Checkley's substitute pro, Riffatulah Mohammed, who dominated the home side's reply with an unbeaten 132, hitting the winning boundary in the final over to secure a one wicket victory amid joyous scenes.

Success continued in 2010 when with Jason Brown as their new professional (65 wickets in the season) the club finished second in the league, gaining promotion.

In 2011 the club gained promotion to the Premier League. A bowling quartet of Jason Brown, Richard Cooper, Iain Carr and Gavin Carr saw Checkley to thirteen wins, a superb effort to celebrate its return to the top sphere.

2012 brought floods of rain and Premier League consolidation; and 2013 earned a third place in the Premier League; while the second eleven gained promotion to the Premier Division B and reached the final of the Talbot Shield.

As a postscript it would be good to mention Don Jones, who died just recently, and who personified supporters of local cricket clubs throughout time with years of selfless service to the noble cause.

Appended is a poem that came to light some 60 years ago and which has always been associated with Checkley cricket; and which reminds us that cricket and poetry are never too far apart from each other.

Checkley Village – end of the cricket season

There is so much, so much whereon to gaze
With happiness; so much the mind can find
Worthy of praise within this quiet place
Where time has left the best of things behind
Amongst the purest joys I ever found
Were welcome, warm and tea and pleasant chat
At friendly cricket on this pleasant ground
That's fielder's ally, bane of every bat.

And evening in the lovely street of yore
That leads you through a gracious train of thought
To stone that sharped the shafts, to yews that bore
To church that blessed the bows of Agincourt.

England's still great while past and future meet
Here in the present, where tradition grows
Around tradition with the fragrance sweet
Of hollyhock and clematis and rose
Where time has left the best of things behind
And better things to be than were before.

Pause long, tread softly, seek and you shall find.

CHURCH EATON CC

Church Eaton Cricket Club

In 1978 Haughton Cricket Club was looking for a new site and subsequently began negotiations for a ground in Church Eaton. As a result the Glebelands Sports Association was formed. There was considerable local opposition to this move and much time had to be devoted to drawing up a constitution to appease everyone before a successful solution was found, this won the support of the Church Eaton parish council and proved to be a huge benefit to the local community, who now particularly appreciate the work of the junior sections.

It was in 1980 that the pivotal steps were taken when the final meeting of Haughton Cricket Club was held and its assets were transferred to the GSA. The club was able to enlist the members of the Remnants, a recently disbanded club; and their presence boosted the club in its first season when the club colours of blue and silver were chosen. These made their reappearance on the club clothing in 2013. 1980 also saw the election of an official junior coach.

It was then that a farmer's field had to be converted into a cricket ground: a huge undertaking at the time. It was only in 1982 that the first game was played at Church Eaton matches having played at Rowley Park in the interim years. At this stage the pavilion was still unfinished and a portacabin and the Village Institute had to be brought into use before the new pavilion was ready for opening in May 1983 when former England, Lancashire and Staffordshire player Jack Ikin brought a team along to mark the occasion.

Before the beginning of the following season a vote was taken about the possibilities of league membership. After the closest of votes and a debate about the most suitable league for the club to join, the North Staffs and District won the day; a big moment in the history of the club, but a vital step given the metamorphosis of local cricket. Saturday friendly games were becoming ever more difficult to arrange as competitive Leagues grew. The decision was to prove the correct one.

In the intervening years Church Eaton CC has enjoyed a great deal of success in the South Cheshire Alliance, Staffordshire Club Cricket Championship and the Stone and District. In the latter competition the club achieved the League and Pinfold double in 2011.

Built on the back of strong consistent performances by a team mostly fed from the junior ranks the club was granted approval to make its inaugural bow in the North Staffordshire and South Cheshire Premier League in the 2012 season. Picturesque Church Eaton is proud of its progress and looks to go from strength to strength with the support of its vibrant community.

CREWE CC

Crewe Vagrants Cricket Club was founded in 1976, as the result of a merger between Crewe LMR and Crewe Vagrants. Crewe LMR's origins go back to 1866 when a group of railway clerks set up a club which they named Crewe Alexandra Cricket Club, settling into their own ground in 1872 and celebrating the first game with a win over Alsager. Two years later the club moved to Earle Street which was to be its home for nearly a hundred years.

Earle Street has the distinction of being along with the Oval the only cricket ground to have housed significant soccer matches. England met Wales at Earle Street in 1888 and there were two F A Cup semi finals played there in the same decade, featuring Blackburn Rovers, Wolverhampton Wanderers, Aston Villa and Glasgow Rangers, grander fare than that on offer at Gresty Road these days.

In 1894, accompanied by Nantwich, the Alexandra Cricket Club elected to join the North Staffordshire and District League, winning the championship in the first season after a playoff with Burslem. In those years clubs were allowed up to two professionals. Crewe declined to use this facility but still went on to win the championship again in 1900 and 1901. Not until 1931 did the club suffer the indignity of relegation, a disappointment soon assuaged when the club immediately took the championship of the second division to find themselves back in the top flight in 1933.

The advent of the Second World War created difficulties for the club in fulfilling its fixtures with the result that an amalgamation was formed with Nantwich, the new club operating as Nantwich Alexandra in the 1940 season. After the war the ownership of the ground passed into the hands of the LMS Railway Company and when fixtures were resumed in 1946, the new club (eventually to be called Crewe LMR) found itself in the second division where it remained for eight seasons before promotion to the first division.

In 1960 the club appointed as its professional the Surrey seam bowler Dennis Cox, a move producing instant success. The club won the North Staffs and District title in successive seasons in 1961 and 1962; following this up by topping the table in the first season of the new North Staffs and South Cheshire League in 1963. Winning the Talbot Cup in 1964 preceded another championship triumph in 1975 – the last year that the club played at Earle Street as Crewe LMR.

After the merger with Crewe Vagrants the club continued to prosper under the captaincy of Alan Jennison when Paul Marshall was the club professional. The junior coaching which had been so successful at Earle Street continued to produce players for the first and second team. John "Animal" Morris who played for Derbyshire, Durham and England came through this system. John was a hugely gifted player who arguably never reached his full potential and is probably best remembered for 'buzzing' up a country game during an Ashes tour in a plane piloted by David Gower.

The Crewe Vagrants Club was originally formed in 1933, so named because the club, not having its own ground, had to play all its matches at opponents' venues. Some land had been purchased in the mid thirties but league cricket came to the site only in the mid seventies when Crewe LMR left Earle Street to take over the running of the cricket section. By that time hockey and squash were also being played at the ground.

The new Shavington bypass took nearly half of the club's land with result that funding from the Highways Agency and Sport England created the opportunity to replace the old wooden clubhouse with new facilities for all the sports being played, the present clubhouse being opened in 1995.

Cricket continues to thrive in Crewe's pleasant Cheshire venue.

ECCLESHALL CC

The first recorded mention of Eccleshall Cricket Club dates to early May 1849 when a group of twenty or thirty men took the decision to bring cricket to the town. A game seems to have been played immediately against a team from Cotes Heath and Standon who won the day.

A name connected with this new venture was a Mr Lyon of Johnson Hall who played a significant role in the early days. He was a Cambridge Blue who represented Staffordshire – Eccleshall's first cricketer of note. He was not the only clergyman to turn out for the club in those days – the Rev Vernon Yongue was another notable; and it is probably the clerical involvement that enabled the first home matches to be played on "land lent by the church". It is possible that this same land is the current site where Eccleshall now plays. The state of the pitches left much to be desired if the scores in the early matches are an accurate assessment. Scores of forty and twenty five were the usual tally even though matches often took place over two Saturdays, home and away, presumably leaving ample time for socialising.

By 1851 the club had found a home on land adjacent to Cross Butts, owned by the Lyon family. Opponents shed light on clubs past and present who were fielding teams in Victorian times: Victoria CC of Stoke on Trent, Trentham CC, Stafford Wednesday, Whitmore, Stafford institute and Birmingham Arcadians. The club is shown to have boasted a flagpole on a map of 1879.

At some unrecorded point the club moved to the field opposite the Newport Road entrance of Johnson Hall and it was there in 1871 that a match was played against Whitmore, ten players per side. Eccleshall batted first and reached a total of seventy five with the evergreen Rev Yongue topscoring with fifteen. Whitmore replied with seventy one. Eccleshall failed in the second innings, mustering only twenty four which left Whitmore the simple task of making twenty nine to win the match by nine wickets. This game was watched by "huge crowd, including many of the fairer sex."

It is interesting to note that many families in and around Eccleshall today can locate their forefathers by the names of Eccleshall's nineteenth century players: Long, Norris, Bennion, Steedon, Edwards, Hopkins, Sharrod, Dempsey and Glennie.

The club were obliged to move home again in the first years of the twentieth century. This time because a reservoir was built underneath the ground. Cricket took place in the field by Fletcher's Garden Centre, then in the field opposite Chester Lodge.

Thereafter the club seems to have entered a period of long decline and surprisingly virtually no history of the club survives until the years following the Second World War. Even then it was only in 1959 when Mark Carter of Eccleshall Castle and Dr Ross Harrison founded the present club. En Tout Cas laid a square and a pavilion was bought from ROF Swynnerton for fifty pounds. Away games only could be played for a while, all on a friendly basis.

An influx of young players from Graham Balfour School and King Edward the Sixth swelled the numbers in the seventies, a second eleven was created and the first junior under eighteen side came into being, the first precursor of junior cricket teams.

1980 marked the club's first foray into league cricket when it joined the new South Cheshire Alliance. It won both divisions in 1983. Many years were spent in the North Staffs and District League before the move was made into the North Staffs and South Cheshire Premier League. The club has just entered a Third Eleven into the Stone League for 2013 and completed its new pavilion in time for the start of the season.

With a complement of seven junior teams, cricket is thriving in this picturesque corner of Staffordshire.

ELWORTH CC

Year 2013 was a double celebration at Elworth: the League's fifty year anniversary coincides with a hundred years of cricket at the Cheshire club.

The story began in October 1913 with a meeting at the home of Alec Palmer and two fellow members of the Elworth Mount Pleasant Methodist Church. The Elworth Mount Pleasant Cricket Club was born with no structure, no ground, no officers, no pavilion, no sightscreens, no players and no fixtures. Things could only improve.

They did. In 1914 a field in the village was used and the first game played. The home side amassed 22 runs (extras top scoring with seven) and the match was lost by 88 runs.

The Great War put a temporary end to cricket; and thereafter, following a few itinerant years, the club found a home on the Boothville ground, which is where games are played today. The rent in those days was just £1 per annum; and there was an interest free loan enabling a wooden pavilion to be constructed.

Cricket ceased again during the Second World War and it was not until 1946 when Elworth resumed with just one team. It was still very much a Methodist chapel club. Sunday cricket was out of the question, alcohol and card games where money was exchanged forbidden. "Soldiers in Satan's army".

In 1964 the club decided on an amicable separation from the chapel and set about raising funds to build the new brick pavilion which, with two added extensions, remains in use today. By now the club had exchanged friendly cricket for membership first of the Cheshire Club Conference, then of the Cheshire Cricket Association. Another change came along in 1976 when the club successfully applied to join the North Staffs and District League. Promotion was followed by a championship win before yet another move, this time to the NSSCL in 1980.

The season of 1984 was to show how far Elworth had progressed when it won the League by a clear nine points .The season was made doubly memorable by winning the Cheshire Cup.

In celebration of the millennium the pavilion was extended, a double bay practice facility installed and an all weather pitch set up on the edge of the square. Then came a new brick score box with an electronic scoreboard and a substantial brick garage to house all the ground equipment. Further cause for celebration is the purchase of the freehold of the ground and an agreement to purchase 0.7 acre field next door so as to provide improved facilities for junior members.

In recalling some of the more notable players in Elworth's past, three come to mind. Bert Sproson was the club's finest batsmen in the years immediately preceding the Second World War. Born in Wheelock in 1915 he was signed, after a career in junior football, by Leeds United, subsequently moving to Tottenham Hotspur who sold him to Manchester City for the then considerable sum of ten thousand pounds. At the age of twenty one he made his debut for England, the first of his eleven caps, with Stanley Matthews on the right wing. Like many of his generation he had a career cruelly cut short by the war.

In 1989, for a game against Knypersley, Elworth hired another of its heroes as a deputy professional. This was New Zealand captain Martin Crowe, then ranked fifth best batsmen in the world. He rewarded the club with a score of seventy nine

Matthew Winter joined Elworth when he was six years old. In 2011, at the age of seventeen, he scored 200 not out against Hem Heath in a second eleven match. Two years later as an Oxford "fresher" he represented his university in the Varsity match to earn him his "blue".

With ownership of the ground, expanding facilities and a supply of good class cricketers Elworth look forward to continued success.

FENTON CC

Anna of the Five Towns made Arnold Bennett's name but did little for the self esteem of Fenton, one of the Potteries' six towns that the great novelist omitted from his books. He had no right to leave the town out. Like its five sisters it had a park, a mayor and a town hall, even if the latter was not quite so well embellished as some of the others. (The oldest Pottery's quip: "Why is Fenton town hall like a sailor's trousers? No ballroom).

Fenton's struggle for identity has helped create a feisty cricket club that boxes well above its weight. It has been in existence since at least 1885 when, as so many other clubs in the league, it had its foundations in the local Methodist church. Its early home was in the grounds of the patrician Great Fenton Hall, owned by the Smith family, and cricket was played there until the hall was demolished in 1900. Happily the land was bequeathed to the people of Fenton and carried the name of Smith's Pool which subsequently became Smithpool Park – the Lido to locals.

The club played at its original location for almost a century on a ground with no pavilion, no electricity and no running water. The club was never a wealthy one and life was often a struggle. Yet success did come its way. In 1899, 1902, 1903 and 1909 the club won the championship of the North Staffs and District League with players of some distinction, particularly H Dearing and E.H.Bourne. The latter was the first Fenton player to be selected in the Staffordshire Minor Counties Eleven where he appeared alongside the great S.F.Barnes.

The club did not move home during the early years but by contrast saw action in several competitions. It was a founder member not only of the North Staffs and District but also of the South Moorlands League and of the Stone and District League. In 1959 Fenton won both Division One and Division Four of the Stone and District League. Two names emerge from that successful time: Ken Kingsbury and Jim Kent: the latter one of the iconic players that every club can hope to boast. He was a Fenton stalwart for many years and was still turning out for his club in his 70th year, while making a considerable contribution to the wider world of local cricket.

The club showed an admirable determination to fight its corner given scant resources and facilities finally improved when the club crossed the park in 1973 to its present position. After nearly a hundred years the club had its own pavilion, lights and water. Work has proceeded since then to build the ground up to its current standard.

The new ground housed games in the Stone League for over twenty years until the members voted for a change in order to match the club with a different set of teams. In 1997 the club elected to join the South Cheshire Alliance. A very happy season ensued but events overcame the South Cheshire which was broken up, its teams going their various ways. Fenton was back in the expanding North Staffs and District League until the last move in 2006 to the North Staffs and South Cheshire League.

The club settled comfortably into its new surroundings and enjoyed welcome success in 2007 by finishing second in Division 3A. By this time Fenton was employing professionals, a far cry from the humble beginnings at Smithpool; and in the runners up season the signing was Indian pace bowler Ashish Zaidi who in a memorable game against Wedgwood took all 10 for just 20 runs. He still holds the league record in the senior sections for the best seasonal average.

Probably the smallest club in the North Staffs and South Cheshire, with a playing membership of only 20 to 30, Fenton has had to fight hard to maintain its status in an area where a number of clubs are growing stronger. The step up to the NSSCL has been at times a challenge which the members have faced head on and found ways to survive. This admirable club's proud motto reflects the community in which it lives: "Onwards and Upwards".

GREAT CHELL CC

In 1960, Great Chell, one of Staffordshire's bedrock clubs, opened a fine new electronic scoreboard. This was soon followed by the building of a stand which could seat seven hundred and fifty spectators. In 1963 Great Chell became one of the founder members of the North Staffs and South Cheshire Cricket League. Bright horizons beckoned.

By 1990 fortunes had changed dramatically. The club resigned from the league; the ground was put up for sale. The club became part of cricket's history.

What are left are the memories of some of the club's finest days and of the remarkable players who have in some way been associated with Great Chell over the years. One of the most outstanding occasions must be the match in 1969 when the North Staffs and South Cheshire League regained the Rothman Trophy by beating the Northern League by 39 runs in the final of the inter-league competition to win the trophy for the second time in four years before a bumper crowd of 3500 spectators. A similar number had watched the first victory in what is now the President's Trophy when the Yorkshire Council were the defeated opponents.

In the game against the Northern League Nasim-ul-Ghani, then Longton's professional and later manager of Pakistan was top scorer with 57 out of a total of 165 besides taking two wickets, though the match winning bowler was Leek's Barry Coates who finished with seven wickets for fifteen. Also in the team that day was Gerry Sobers, brother of Garry.

It's fitting to name the triumphant eleven who represented the league on that memorable occasion. Arthur Sutton (Newcastle and Hartshill); Nasim-ul-Ghani (Longton); Barry Coates (Leek); Vic Babb (Porthill Park); Geoff Hardstaff (Newcastle and Hartshill); Gerry Sobers (Norton); Brian Jackson (Knypersley); Bill Taylor (Leek); Peter Howell (Bignall End); Les Lowe (Knypersley); David Brock (Newcastle and Hartshill).

Great Chell's story is populated by a host of notable characters. Peter Gibbs and Peter Hampson were two influential players in the 60's, the latter a more than useful medium pacer, a Hanley High School boy, as was Peter Gibbs who went on to have a successful career with Derbyshire.

Hampson can recall many happy times and outstanding players in his time at the club. One of his favourites was Trevor Goddard, the South African, who was the professional for some seasons. Goddard had already earned a mention in Jim Laker's book "Over To Me". The great England off-spinner had spotted him as a sixteen year old in Durban where he was coaching. To quote Peter: "It was a thrill to play alongside Trevor Goddard, he instilled confidence into his teammates and showed tremendous concentration. In fact, in those 1960's days there were two of the game's gentlemen playing cricket in North Staffordshire, Trevor Goddard and John Ikin.

On one occasion when Great Chell was playing against Crewe LMR they came up against the ex- Surrey bowler Dennis Cox who was enjoying a good day. Peter, a left hand bat, joined Trevor Goddard to put together a rearguard action. "I remember vividly Trevor coming down the wicket after every ball I faced," says Peter. "He told me to keep playing straight and make sure that I used 'soft hands' to take the pace off the ball. His encouragement gave me a surge of confidence and we held out."

Peter has a typical story about John Ikin. Bignall End were visitors for an important end of the season game. Trevor Goddard had carried his bat through the Great Chell innings and asked Peter to open the bowling. He bowled a ball which lifted off just short of a length which flicked John's glove on the way through to the wicket keeper. John did not wait for the umpire's verdict. He walked immediately.

Great Chell spread its cricketing net in the 1960's, visiting clubs from other leagues. Peter relished the experience of these excursions. "I remember going to Rawtenstall in the Lancashire League. Sonny Ramadhin, the great West Indian spin bowler, was their professional. I was amazed at the zip he put on the ball as it flew up off the pitch. He kept his sleeves rolled down and kept on his maroon West Indian cap when he bowled. Great Chell was widening its cricketing horizons."

Sadly, Goddard's son suffered from asthma, a condition not helped by the English climate and Trevor had to return to South Africa. He was much missed; but was replaced by what Peter calls "the calypso beat orchestrated by the fastest bowler in the world, Wesley Hall."

Peter goes on:" The problem that Wes came up against when he came into league cricket was that he pitched the ball too short. It either flew over the stumps or found an edge, The ferocious pace of the ball meant that catches went down on a regular basis even though the slips were pushed back to the boundary."

Peter adds the sequel. The Great Chell team sat down with Wes, advising him to pitch the ball up. He accepted the advice graciously, realising that it might be a useful ploy in league cricket and he soon reaped the rewards with regular hauls of wickets.

The appointment of Dennis Cox as club professional totally changed the outlook of the club. After taking senior nets on Friday evenings Dennis would coach the juniors on Saturday mornings. He worked tirelessly to improve dramatically the technique of any player who sought his advice allowing everyone to reach his full potential senior players were offered the same help. One to avail himself was Trevor Blank who was later to become a professional with Silverdale.

Sadly Dennis had to retire after suffering a heart attack but his work bore fruit: the following year the First Eleven took the League title. Brian James, another all round professional, was captain that year and the win was dedicated to Dennis who had nurtured a priceless team ethic in the club.

The large facility that was Chell's ground began inexorably to take its toll on the club's finances. The club was eventually sold with the aim of cricket being played on the same site for a further five years. Alas this idea did not come to fruition. There was a brief period when the club joined with Sneyd before the inevitable happened.

Great Chell has written a mighty chapter in the history of Staffordshire cricket... The unique memories remain.

HANFORD CC

Villagers who worked on the Duke of Sutherland's estate formed the cricket club in 1892 and in the following year arranged their first match against Longton Wesleyans yet another team based around a Methodist chapel. Games took place in "an alliance of junior clubs in the North Staffs area".

By 1896 Trentham, Keele, Tittensor, Middleport, Crewe Free Church and Burslem were fielding teams in the Alliance. In that year The Duke made a gift of land in Wilson Road which afforded the luxury of a flat cricket ground and room for a football pitch, tennis courts, a bowling green and a village hall. The Sutherlands took a benevolent interest in the development of the cricket club. An article in the Sentinel read "The pavilion, which his Grace the Duke has given to the Hanford club is now in course of erection and many willing helpers have been busy this week to show their appreciation to (sic) the privilege his Grace has so kindly bestowed." The Sentinel knew its place

In the 1930's large parts of the Trentham estate were sold off and the villagers were offered the chance to buy all the playing fields and the village hall at the knock-down price of fifty pounds. Surprisingly only the hall was purchased with the result that the land was sold to Stoke City Council for housing development. An opportunity missed.

The club was deprived of its home but was rescued by a local landowner who provided some land off Church Lane. Unfortunately the land fell some thirty feet from top to bottom with a flat piece centrally sited that served as a square. Nevertheless the club soldiered on and continued playing up to and after the Second World War, when it joined the Stone and District League. The ground was still a farmer's field; in use most of the time for cattle grazing, with a square fenced off and an outfield cut when the farmer "had the time".

In the early 1950's the owner of the land and club president Bill Tellwright died and with his death came the need to quit the ground. Negotiations were well under way with Trentham Cricket Club in the Park when an unexpected windfall came in the form of a clause in Mr Tellwright's will which left the ground to the club "for the playing of cricket in the summer and football in the winter." The club now owned the ground and was free to carry out whatever improvements it wished. No more grazing rights, no longer a fenced off square. Instead a machine to cut the outfield and sight screens (which had to be pushed from Trentham one Sunday morning along the A34).

The club won several honours in the 50's but by the next decade player retirements were taking their toll and with the club seemingly unable to attract new blood the club was relegated from Division One of the league. The club carried on however in a positive way, improving facilities in the pavilion and opening a bar. An all too common modern example of vandalism saw the new pavilion badly damaged by fire in 1975, but the club responded by building even better facilities.

In 1978 the club caused a stir in local cricket circles by applying to join the North Staffs and District Cricket League. Political wrangling almost left the club high and dry without a competition to play in until after much discussion it was admitted into Section "B". A club professional, at five pounds per match was set on. John Phillips stayed with the club for several seasons. He later tragically lost his life in a road accident. The club joined the NSSCL in 2006.

The club has an eye for the future and is developing a youth policy which goes from strength to strength; and looks forward to many happy and successful seasons in the North Staffs and South Cheshire League.

HEM HEATH CC

HEM HEATH C.C.

Hem Heath Cricket Club is relatively new member of the North Staffs and Cheshire Cricket League, winning promotion only in 2003, fifty one years after starting life as Stafford and Hem Heath Colliery on a ground very close to the present venue. For many years opponents such as Wood Lane, Checkley and Moddershall were encountered in the Stone League. Facilities were shared with bowls, tennis and football.

In the late 1970's the club moved to a new location close to the Hem Heath colliery site on the Trentham Road. At this time the club had no pavilion it could call its own as it was just part of the sports and social sector. Players changed in rooms underneath the social club buildings, certainly offering a unique experience to visiting teams.

This was a time of great success in the Stone League, culminating in 1979 with a clean sweep of all the Stone League honours: first and second eleven champions, the Pinfold Cup, the Bailey Shield and the Hassell Trophy.

In the early 80's the club was allowed to build a small pavilion and changing rooms enabling players to abandon the subterranean arrangements. This new facility proved a great bonus to developing the family involvement which features strongly in Hem Heath.

In the late 80's great hardship was caused far and wide by the demise of the coal industry. One of the many victims of the pit closures was the Hem Heath social club and members had hurriedly to devise a means of survival. Yet despite these severe difficulties it was at this time that the club gained promotion to the North Staffs and District League with successful further promotion to Senior "B" in the early 90's when the club also won the League Knockout Trophy.

Towards the end of the 90's the regeneration project put forward by Stoke City Council required the club to seek relocation. After much discussion the club's home was moved to the north end of Trentham Lakes close by Stoke City Football Club. Portacabins were the order of the day at first both for changing facilities and for social events but these temporary provisions still afforded space for many happy celebrations for club members.

Success on the playing side coincided with the building of a new pavilion and promotion into the North Staffs and Cheshire League in 2003. In the following year the club finished as runners up to Moddershall in the Staffordshire Cup. In 2008 the club won promotion to the Premier Division where its best achievement thus far has been to finish in third spot in 2011.

Thanks to the hard work of all its members, players and ground staff the club now owns its new ground and pavilion. Numerous three day county games have been hosted as a result. There are ten junior sides, from under 9's to under 17's and many of the juniors have gone on to represent their county.

Many of the club's members have been with Hem Heath for over thirty years while the Club Executive, Chairman and Secretary have seen over forty years' service. The club is very proud to be a part of the North Staffs and South Cheshire League and offers congratulations on its fiftieth anniversary.

KIDSGROVE CC

Records show that the club was playing in 1874 under the name of Kidsgrove Alexander and that the team was made up mostly of railway workers. At some point it changed its name to Clough Hall Cricket Club; and in 1963 changed once more to Kidsgrove Cricket Club. In that year, under the captaincy of Rob Malkin, the club carried off the Championship of the North Staffs and District League with Stan Crump, then aged 53, topping the League bowling averages at a remarkable 5.5 runs per wicket.

In 1979 the club moved its home to the present Kinnersley Ground and joined the North Staffs and South Cheshire League in 1981. In more recent times the best performance by a Kidsgrove player was also in the 1979 season when Peter Gill was the leading batsman in the Senior "A" Section of the NSDCL scoring 946 runs, a feat bettered only in the preceding 50 years by Frank Worrall and John Ikin.

The club's most significant achievement is probably being responsible for the formation of the Kidsgrove Junior League in 1947 which provided Monday evening matches for boys under 18 years old. Farley, Hurst, Davenport and Fryer are four names closely connected with the foundation of this competition, now The R. Cherry Kidsgrove and District Junior Cricket League after Bob Cherry who served as its Secretary for 42 years, this junior league has been a huge and continuing success story.

The club has currently three senior teams, five junior teams and an under 13 women's eleven.

KNYPERSLEY CC

Knypersley C.C.

Since its formation in 1880 Knypersley Cricket Club has been one of the leading clubs in North Staffordshire. A long and illustrious association with the North Staffs and District League preceded becoming a founder member of the North Staffs and South Cheshire League in 1963.

In the early 1950's the club hired an unknown young fast bowler as a professional. This was Frank Tyson who's raw pace induced Knypersley's long serving wicket keeper Levi Lowe to stand further back than for any other bowler he had encountered. Northamptonshire quickly snapped him up and by 1955 he was part of Len Hutton's successful ashes winning side in Australia, taking ten wickets in the match in Melbourne followed by a further nine in Sydney. Coincidentally another member of that victorious squad was Bob Appleyard, a Yorkshire immortal, who made his debut for his county in a second eleven game at Knypersley, taking fifteen Staffordshire wickets.

In the first year of NSSCL's formation Knypersley had great hopes of winning the title for the first time; but after playing only two games club professional Brian Jackson was signed by Derbyshire. In those days substitute professionals were not allowed and the club had to perforce carry on without one in the side. After an impressive first class career with Derbyshire Brian Jackson returned to Tunstall Road in 1969 for a further four year stint as professional; and in 1970 claimed 66 league wickets at a cost of just 7.24, a league record which still stands.

Current first class umpire Rob Bailey was a local lad who followed his father John into the Knypersley team before going on to Northants to enjoy an outstanding first class career which brought him 4 England test caps. He subsequently moved to Derbyshire where he ended his playing days. Another Knypersley youngster is Robert Frost (son of club stalwart Ivan) who graduated to Warwickshire as wicket keeper and who is now member of its coaching team.

Knypersley's overseas players include brothers Qaiser and Nayyar Abbas, both of whom have played their part in helping the club win trophies. Australian Mark Tournier's excellent six year spell at Tunstall Road ensured another of the club's successes while Darren Long was another outstanding player to lead Knypersley to the title a feat repeated by South African pace man Brian Gessner. Home grown players to prosper include long serving Neil Dutton, the club's all time wicket taker, and Les Lowe who amassed more runs than any other player in the club's history.

Since 1946 the Knypersley ground has hosted Staffordshire's Minor County fixtures and has frequently been used for representative matches. In addition the ground has become an occasional home venue for Derbyshire in one day games, giving the locals the chance to see Holding, Kapil Dev, Hick, Malcolm, Willey, Agnew, John Morris and Kim Barnett, the latter turning out later for the club in the NSSCL in 2008/9.

Knypersley Cricket Club continues to develop, with a strong vibrant youth section to support the senior sides. Off the field the refurbished Vice President's suite provides an excellent facility for members, sponsors and visiting teams while the top quality four lane nets opened in 2012 ensure that the club continues to progress, guaranteeing that Knypersley will remain one of the leading cricket clubs in the area.

LEEK CC

This old market town, Arnold Bennett's Axe, now an antiques centre, situated in the Moorlands, always requires a good trip from its league visitors.

The club was formed in 1844, moving to its current home in 1866. Arthur Shrewsbury (W G Grace's favourite cricketer: "Give me Arthur") played several times as the club's professional as did William Bates, the first English player to take a test match hat-trick. Leek joined the North Staffs League in 1893 but in 1894 came a split, thus creating two separate clubs, Leek Highfield and Leek CC. They reunited after the war as Leek CC, playing at Highfield. The club passed through various ups and downs, a revival coming with the appointment of England's greatest ever bowler, Sidney Barnes, who became coach in 1937. Bert Shardlow was appointed club professional in 1946 and in nine spectacular seasons took 855 league wickets at 7.74 each. With other key players such as Boulton, Horden, Crump and Turner, Leek had a very strong team during the post-war years. They took the championship in 1947, and were runners up in 1948, 1950 and 1951.

The 1950's saw a decline in the club's playing fortunes but 1954 was a historic year for Leek Cricket Club when the ground at Highfield was purchased from Mr. John Tatton, the then owner of Highfield Hall. The purchase price was £3,000, and to offset the financial burden the Club decided to sell their second ground at Beggars Lane for £1,100. Relegation came in 1960 and successes came along rarely until the mid 70's when the club won the league championship. That came in 1974 when the enigmatic Brian Tatton captained the First Eleven with a team blessed with a collection of very fine players that kept his side in contention for honours. In the 1980's the two talented Sri Lankans Athol Samaraskena and Granville da Silva played for the club when by this time the captaincy had passed to Dave Cartledge. The following year Dave became the club's professional and enjoyed an outstanding career scoring profusely for club and county, hitting in 1982 what was then the club's fastest century (in 82 balls) and setting a new league record of 1102 runs in 1987. In the same period Steve Bailey notched up a century at Lord's playing for the National Association of Young Cricketers.

The late 80's were marked by the loss of several long serving stalwarts, particularly Derrick Turner, Joan Fisher, Stan Hutchinson and Pat Charnock. Then in 1990 the club's fortunes again took a much needed turn when in an unforgettable season, with the club crowned league champions and triumphing in the Staffs Cup, the team could boast the unique record of having a father and three sons play in the same team. Leek also won the Talbot Cup in 1991 and 1992 and the Staffs Cup again in 1994.

With the new millennium came a fresh resurgence. The West Indian, Ottis Gibson, was part of the remarkable achievement in 2001 when the club won the League, the Talbot Cup and the Staffs Cup, a wonderful treble, not achieved before or since. Leek engaged some very accomplished professionals in recent years; these included the following internationals Albie Morkel, Alfonso Thomas, Vasbert Drakes, Kim Barnett and Tino Best. Leek continues to enjoy success right up to the present day celebrating as Premier Division Champions in both 2012 and 2013.

Leek has long been the eastern outpost of North Staffordshire cricket with a proud history of success over long years.

LEYCETT CC

Leycett is one of hundreds of clubs throughout the land that can claim to owe its creation to the mining industry. Coal had been extracted at Leycett since at least the beginning of the eighteenth century and with the sinking of four shafts ("Bang Up" and "Fair Lady) around 1860 the village population grew as did the new mining community of Madeley Heath a few miles down Leycett Lane. At that time cricket started to be played: a welcome distraction from the hazardous life below ground with its frequent collapses and explosions.

The first recorded cricket match took place in 1892 and four years later the club joined the North Staffs Combination League. Two teams were playing by the early 1900's and the club's progress was marked by a signal success in 1911 when it won the First division of the league, a feat it repeated the following year. Two protagonists of the day left their mark: the Clarke brothers both noted all rounders.

The First World War saw cricket at Leycett in abeyance. It resumed in peacetime when the club, after a further season in the Combination, joined the North Staffs and District League. Unfortunately the club found it difficult to put two teams in the field and in the mid twenties the membership of the league was revoked. A new home was found in the Fenton League where in 1926 the club won the Sentinel Shield. In 1928 the club went into the Tunstall and District League, leaving the vacant slot in the Fenton League to the second eleven.

War again put a stop to cricket in the village, a bleak time followed by an explosion of enthusiasm by men keen to return to the club and to resume playing. Jack Hill was a towering figure at this time. Jack played his first game for the club in 1908 with myriad roles: club captain, management member, labourer, player (his final appearance in 1960). An overman at the colliery, Don organised the first sponsorship for the club which purchased them much needed equipment and made massive efforts to further the fortunes of the club, which were recognised by his appointment to President in the mid sixties.

Then, in 1955, things began to change. The life of the pit, the source of so much of the club's existence, was drawing to a close. Winning the Bailey Shield in 1957 might well have been the club's last hurrah as the disappearance of the colliery drained much of the life out of the village with people leaving to live, work and indeed play their cricket elsewhere.

Thanks to enthusiasm and good management the worst did not happen. Leycett rejoined the North Staffs and District League where the club spent the next ten seasons. During that time application was made to the landlord and then Club President Quentin Crewe to buy the ground. Permission was also successfully sought to build a brand new club building. The club's first professional was signed: Philip Wrench, who has since made league history by becoming its first deputy sheriff in the state of Florida. He still keeps in daily touch with the cricket in England via the police computer.

In 1975 the junior team won its first title, the League Knock out and then did it again the following year. In 1989 the team won its first Kidsgrove league title. Success for the 1st eleven came in 1990 when with Dean Headley as professional; the club won promotion to the top division by virtue of finishing in runners up position along with a victory in the Talbot Cup competition. Alas, relegation was the club's fate in the following season...

By 1996 it was becoming clear that the club was no longer able to rely on the next generation of players being born and bred in the village now that the pit had closed the club set about building a youth policy. By 1998 there had been established under 11's, 13's., 15's and 18's. This meant an eventual increase in membership. In 2001 a Sunday senior team entered the Stone League and eight years later a fourth eleven was formed.

In 2008 a new electronic score box was constructed along with all weather net facilities and in the same year promotion was won, as champions, to the Premier League. As before the team was relegated after just one season but there is no doubt of the good health of the Leycett club which will continue to compete at a high level.

LITTLE STOKE CC

LITTLE STOKE C.C.

The cricket ground at Little Stoke takes the stranger by surprise. It lodges firmly on the hillside, sweeping up from the valley of the Trent. One first casual glance suggests it to be an unusual and unsuitable site for a cricket ground. It is only when the visitor ventures the ground and looks back across the playing area towards the distant valley floor that the full splendour is revealed.

Despite the relatively recent intrusion of new housing development up and along the Uttoxeter Road which forms the Aston Lodge estate the overall scene is still one of considerable charm. As the eye sweeps down the valley parts of Stone, Walton, the village and church of Aston and the hamlet of Little Aston in the near distance can all be picked out. Today it is a very open place, almost bereft of the hedges and trees that once gave the ground its intimate atmosphere.

A smart brick and tile pavilion stands solidly in the corner of the main ground, boasting a modern bar, clubroom, changing rooms, showers and toilets. Opposite is to be found the main score box blending proudly with the surrounding scene. This doubles up as the home of the machinery and equipment vital to the cricket, priceless assets for the club. Sight screens, covers, practice area and carefully thought out parking facilities along with the wooden pavilion on the top ground and the bowling green between the two complete the picture.

It is however the ground itself that takes the eye of the practised cricketer. Despite the slope on the main ground it gives good drainage and drying capabilities in wet weather. The outfield is fast, the square firm and flat. More importantly over the years it has invariably produced high quality batting wickets that still afford bowlers plenty of chance to shine. For many years the wickets have been exceptional for their pace and bounce.

Little Stoke is a club believing in self help and has made steady progress thanks in large measure to members willing to give of their time. An outstanding example is former secretary and club captain Sid Jenkins. The club has named the ground after him.

The club was established in 1946 by the amalgamation of Aston by Stone and Stone Christ Church. Improvements were gradually made to the ground and in 1965 the club hosted their first Minor Counties match. In 1979 the club joined the North Staffs and South Cheshire League. Promotion to Division One in 1994 was followed by championship success in 1998.

Promotion to the Premier Division was achieved in 2002; and two years later

Shahid Afridi was setting a new league record with the fastest century off fifty balls in forty five minutes against Stone. Promotion and relegation alternated during the first years of this century but the club has now returned to the Premier Division.

The ground continues to undergo improvement, expansion and development. Very significant is the junior development programme with sides in the u9, u11, u13 and u17 with integration into senior sides, producing many players for Staffordshire. Alan Richardson, recently one of Wisden's five Cricketers of the Year and who enjoyed a first class career with Derbyshire, Middlesex, Worcestershire and the England Lions came through the ranks at Little Stoke.

Non progredi est regredi. "Not to advance is to go back." - A philosophy to inspire future members and players of Little Stoke for years to come.

LONGTON CC

There was a time when the intrepid traveller, passing through the architectural delights of Dresden and Florence would eventually light up at Cocknage, the erstwhile home of Longton Cricket Club. Could any cricket club in the world boast a more illustrious approach? However in 1951 the club forsook these patrician neighbours and moved to nearby Blurton, though the Cocknage pavilion went along too.

This was not the first occasion on which the club had moved grounds. It began life as least as early as 1891 as Dresden Church Cricket Club, situated on the higher ground South and West of Lane End (or Longton as the modernists name it) overlooking and avoiding the choking smoke of the town. It was a creation of the local public school men and was financed largely by wealthy pottery manufacturers whose houses were located in the affluent suburbs of Ricardo Street and Queens Park.

The new century brought with it a new ground. The Duke of Sutherland released land for a public park and a new and attractive cricket facility was laid out in ground that had become available. Funds had been raised to allow this successful move with enough left over to build a new pavilion.

The passing years saw the club's reputation grow to become one of the leading and most consistent performers in the North Staffs League. It continued to play at the Cocknage ground which it came to share with Stoke on Trent Rugby Club and to attract large crowds to its games, many of which were much anticipated and hard fought local derbies.

By the beginning of the 1950's the club's expansion brought the need for larger facilities. Accordingly a new venue was found on the Trentham Road on land owned by the City Council, leaving the old historic site to housing development, a frequent sad fate for our cricket grounds. Luckily Longton survived and the Lord Mayor of Stoke, Alderman Horace Barks, declared the new ground open in 1951.

From its inception on the new site the club has made rapid progress and is rightly judged as one of the premier clubs in the North Staffs and South Cheshire League which it joined as a founder member in 1963. With sizeable crowds attending its weekly fixtures the club has been able to set on high class professionals and to develop superb facilities of in-house cricket coaching.

It would be remiss not to list some of Longton's fine achievements over the years. Champions in 1966, 1968, 1969, 1970, 1972, 1977, 1987, 2003, 2004, 2005 and 2009 A formidable record not bettered by any other club and also containing two hat tricks of wins. The Second Elevens have shadowed their seniors well winning their competitions six times. Some individual performances are noteworthy including Andy Clarke's annus mirabilis in 1996 when he captured 104 wickets, still a Premier Division record today and a superb return by Roger De Ville taking all 10 Leek wickets for 37 runs in 1969.

Longton has won the Talbot Cup five times, the Shield six times as well as the Staffordshire Cup and the 20/20 competition.

An impressive list of professionals is written in the club's archives: Nasim-Ul-Ghani, Derek Morgan, Keith Stride, Alfonso Thomas, and Nathan Astle, probably the most notable of a distinguished series. All have been ready to come to this leading Staffordshire club which not surprisingly has accumulated a history of top class fixtures. India, the West Indies, South Africa and Australia have all appeared at Trentham Road. To date 40 minor counties games have been hosted there.

The club is ECB Club mark accredited and has a thriving junior section for all ages from under nines upwards. The baton will be passed to these young cricketers to maintain the highest standards of a club which has never played outside any of the top divisions of the myriad historic structures of the local leagues.

MEAKINS CC

J and G Meakin was an English pottery company founded in 1851. It was based in Hanley

In the nineteenth century J and G Meakin was known for the vast quantities of cheap ironstone china it produced for the domestic English market and for export to Australia, Canada, New Zealand and the United States.

In the early nineteen fifties the company decided to build a cricket ground for its employees. By the early sixties the team was playing in the Stone League with Frank Foster as one of its first captains. Charlie Brooks, Jack Manning and Harold Prince were also leading figures in the club at that time.

From the mid nineteen sixties through to the seventies Meakins enjoyed a string of successful seasons winning a host of Stone League Titles and Cups. In the first eight years of the Pinfold Trophy Meakins emerged seven times as the victors. The Bailey Shield, the Hassall cup and the Charity Shield also came the club's way in those years. Success continued into the nineteen eighties under the captaincy of Robert Brunt and vice captain Ron Watkiss with more league and cup victories; and on the social front with the addition of a bar to the clubhouse.

In 1985 Meakins resigned from the Stone League and applied to join the North Staffs and District Cricket League. The application proved unsuccessful and in the following year the club was forced to reapply to the Stone League. Re-admittance was granted on the condition that the club would be obliged to play in the lower division. The club responded to the challenge by winning the division at the first attempt, so returning to the top echelon. The Stone League then formed a Premier Division and Meakins duly became the first champions.

Dave Kettle was elected chairman of the club in the early eighties and under his watch the club progressed by gaining promotion to the North Staffs and District League. Under the pyramid system the club played in the Stone League and the North Staffs and District League in both "A" and "B" Divisions and won the League Cup.

In 1990 the club purchased a large scout hut from Great Chell, which with the help of many members was transported to Meakins ground and which for twelve months served just as changing rooms. In the next year Eastwood Hanley Football Club was approached for a temporary bar, now replaced by a new modern one.

In 2006 Meakins moved into the North Staffs and South Cheshire League when it merged with the North Staffs and District League. Life in the new

surroundings began in Division Three and continued with progression through to Division Two and then, in 2013, under the captaincy and chairmanship of James Menzies, to promotion to the Premier Division.

Major improvements have been brought about at the ground. The changing rooms have been improved; the clubhouse has been refurbished; the playing area brought to a high standard under the care of senior groundsman Ron Watkiss.

Finally, mention must be made of the junior section which operates under the Academy director Matt Cope. This is a thriving enterprise with nine junior teams ready for the coming season.

All at "Meaks" are looking forward to the future with great hopes and expectations.

MEIR HEATH CC

The history of Meir Heath Cricket Club sheds some light on the story of this club on the Southern confines of the city which was elected to the North Staffs and South Cheshire League in 1996.

Men and women returning home at the end of the Second World War determined to set up a cricket club and had the luck to find in the locality a garage owner, Mr Bartlam, who was happy to offer a field behind his premises for the playing of home fixtures. The enthusiasm and energy of the club's founders were rewarded in 1947 with a place in the Blythe Bridge and Uttoxeter Cricket League.

The club was blessed with ambitious members and a move to larger premises was effected in 1962. Hilderstone Road was the new venue, a ground owned by the late lamented Joules Brewery who exacted an annual rent of £25. Games were now being played in the Stone and District League before yet another move to the North Staffs and District Cricket League marking the club's consistent ambitions to progress its cricketing standards.

After 17 years the club called time on the brewery and moved to Willow Lane, where the first wickets were pitched on April 18th 1980. Soft drinks only to wet the baby's head: the bar licence arrived in May.

Meir Heath can be said to owe its existence to the hard work and dedication of generations of its supporters, who through good times and bad have sought to create a peerless amenity for all to share. Herculean efforts have brought the club from humble beginnings to the wonderful modern amenities at Willow Lane which has hosted minor counties cricket against Suffolk, Lincolnshire and Shropshire.

Older supporters will remember with affection characters such as the rotund wicket keeper, Jack Wyatt, who would console a struggling batsman with "The Lord is my Shepherd I shall not want"; then with a racing tip and advice to bet on the football pools. Cliff Baskeyfield, a Burma Star veteran was for many years the Man Friday of the club, while Aberdonian Dr Law, a specialist in pewter, but not in cricket, became President and Chairman and left his footprint everywhere in Meir Heath CC. When he died at the age of 69 he bequeathed a five figure sum to the club. Frank Winfield's pavilion is dedicated to him.

Since 1996 further development has gone ahead at the club with new nets, an electronic fascia for the scorebox, the addition of a conservatory to the pavilion, a complete renovation of the shower room and an innovative scheme for the harvesting of rainwater: all achieved with the wholehearted support of the members, who into the bargain supplemented the necessary funds obtained from outside sources.

Meir Heath boasts a current League record holder in Neil Crump (of local cricketing family dynasty), Neil's batting average for the matches he played in Division 1B in 2010 was 103.

Meir Heath holds the ECB Clubmark Accreditation and boasts 3 men's senior teams, a women's senior team and 6 junior teams across ages from u9 to u17 for boys and girls.

Meir Heath CC established Women's and Girls cricket teams in 2005. The Women's team is a previous winner of the Midland league and the Midland Cup. Five of its players have represented England and in 2013, Steph Butler was selected for the England U/19's team and Danni Wyatt and Georgia Elwiss both represented the England Women's team. Meir Heath Girls have been Midland Lady Taverner champions on three occasions at U/11, U/13 and U/15's and Staffordshire champions every year since 2005. Many of the girls who played in the first girl's team set up in 2005 are now playing in the current Women's team.

MODDERSHALL CC

It was in 1921 when a young man reluctantly left his home town of Ripon in Yorkshire to come and live and work in the village of Moddershall. Percy Metcalf was a Yorkshire farmer's son, an avid Yorkshire supporter who rarely missed a county game. When he arrived in the Staffordshire village he quickly realised that what was missing was a cricket team and he soon decided to resolve the situation.

Early in 1922 a meeting was held in the Moddershall clubroom with the founding fathers, Percy Gilbert, Captain Johnson, Jack Adderley and Arthur Stubbs who recognised the lack of cricket in the village and formed a plan of campaign. Finding a ground was the first thing on the agenda and as luck would have it a local farmer, Arthur Stubbs, made a field available for games at no charge to the club. There was no shortage of potential players in the village and work to prepare the ground started almost immediately.

For the first few years Moddershall was content with friendly cricket. A thirst for more competitive sport developed and with the encouragement of Percy Schofield the club became one of the founder members of the Stone and District League. The league ceased to operate during the war when the club managed to play friendly games. After the war ended the club was re-formed.

In 1960 the club suffered a setback when the farmer who owned the cricket field served the club notice to quit. However the Director of Spot Acre Nurseries, Frank Hill, heard of the club's plight and offered the use of the Barnfields ground which members were glad and grateful to take up. Members pulled together and set to work on readying their new home and in May 1962 the ground was officially opened by Frank Hill who bowled the first ball to the President, Mr W.R. Midwinter before a match between the first and second elevens.

In 1994 a second ground was purchased, Wrekin View, well named and commanding panoramic views across Staffordshire and Shropshire towards the Welsh mountains. Both grounds are little short of a thousand feet above sea level.

Moddershall joined the North Staffs and District Cricket League in 1975 and in 1989 the North Staffs and South Cheshire Premier League.

From humble beginnings Moddershall C.C has thrived and now boasts a vibrant junior section. Junior cricket has been played at the club since the early 1970's when the matches were played on a friendly basis with the team being ferried to matches in a milk van. However in the early 1980's the club joined the Kidsgrove and District Cricket League since when the junior section has flourished. Now the academy has over one hundred members whose ages range from five to seventeen and the club has players from all the age groups playing for Staffordshire Young Cricketers. Club players have also played Midlands Representative cricket and Sam Kelsall has England under 19 honours.

In recent years the club has had some well known international players on its books, notably Imran Tahir and Rangana Herath. In 1992 when Moddershall were playing against Leycett in Division 1 Section "B" T.Azam scored the fastest century in the League in just 41 minutes and faced only 38 deliveries. The club has won the Premier Division title on 3 occasions in 1997, 1999 and 2008 and Moddershall "A" has won the Division Three "A" title on 2 occasions in 2007 (first season in the NSSCL) and in 2009.

Second and third generations of founder and longstanding members are now featuring at the club which is reaping the benefits of its academy.

Carpe diem. Seize the day. A splendid motto for this forward looking club.

NANTWICH CC

The earliest records of Nantwich's excursions onto the cricket fields of the 1840's are, not surprisingly, a little hazy. First references to cricket in Nantwich suggest that the Club was first known as Nantwich Albion.

It seems that matches were played on Kingsley Fields – not the fine ground of later years, but an adjoining field, and not always on Saturdays, but on Mondays. Saturday was a busy day in the Town's shoe and clothing factories, but Monday was the recognised day of rest, which was the time those early sporting heroes came out to play. Records also suggest that the Monday "day off" was not shared by all the Town's neighbours, so it was not always easy to arrange fixtures.

By 1890 Nantwich was ready for League cricket and the Club's long – though not unbroken association with the North Staffordshire League began. The first record of winning a competitive trophy came in 1895 when the Club won the Junior "A" League.

A few years later, the team dropped out of League cricket to concentrate once more on friendly games.

In 1921, on the Club's return to the North Staffordshire League they won the Senior "B" Championship and were promoted to the Senior "A" section. Nantwich had a scare the following Season when it retained its "A" status only after a play-off with Burslem. But the Club's first heyday was not far off.

Between 1927–1933 Nantwich won the Senior "A" section no less than five times, including the hat-trick of 1927, 1928 and 1929. Then in 1932 Dick Tyldesley the Lancashire and England bower, joined the Club, a capture which warranted "cricket sensation" headlines in those far off days. Tyldesley played for two seasons, helping to secure two more Championships.

In 1934 another famous name joined Nantwich as professional Worcester player, Vic Fox, who was also a noted full-back with Middlesbrough. Fox stayed for five seasons, Nantwich again notching up a Championship in 1937.

It was not all plain sailing for the Club in those apparently halcyon days. In 1935 for instance, the Pavilion on Kingsley Fields and a considerable amount of equipment, was destroyed by fire. But the excellent spirit which abounded in those days ensured that by the start of the 1936 season, a new Pavilion was ready and waiting.

For two seasons 1954 and 1955 Nantwich engaged a former captain of India as its professional G.S. Ramchand – Ram to the cricketing world. In his first season Ram steered the Club to its ninth Senior "A" Championship title scoring 816 runs and taking 60 wickets.

The Club lost the battle to retain the Kingsley Fields ground and in 1956 moved to Council owned Barony Park until moving to their new home at Whitehouse Lane in 1971.

In1963 Nantwich became a founder member of the new North Staffs and South Cheshire League but had to wait until 1980 for its next Championship success. That proved to be the beginning of a hugely successful period for the Club.   It won the title again the next season and was runners-up the following season and then took the title once more in 1983, with West Indian fast bowler Vanburn Holder spearheading the attack.

No glossary on Nantwich Cricket Club could be compiled without recording the deeds of Geoff Bull, Geoff first marched to the wicket for Nantwich in 1934. He played his last game in 1980! In this period there is no doubt that he scored more runs than any batsman whoever played in North Staffordshire and South Cheshire cricket. One innings he played against Frank "Typhoon" Tyson, who just a year later was ripping the heart out of the Aussie batting line up "down under" Geoff made just over 50 and every time the Typhoon dropped one short, the ball thumped into the fence square on the offside. Geoff's innings of 103 made against Freddie Taylor just a few days after he had taken six for thirty-odd against the Australian tourists was, he says, the best knock he ever played.

He was a phenomenon.

The long links with North Staffordshire cricket were finally broken at the end of the 1995 Season when Nantwich opted to play in the Cheshire County competition.

NEWCASTLE AND HARTSHILL CC

The club has its roots in Harpfields Cricket Club, founded in 1921 by Cuthbert Heppell Morley ("Bert" or "The Guv") who was destined to become one of the longest serving secretaries in local club cricket. All his four sons played first team cricket for the club as well as serving on its committee. Strange to relate, the only match in which all the brothers featured was an away fixture against City works at Finney Gardens where play was stopped by a straying wallaby. Bert's grandson currently chairs the club and several of his great grandchildren represent Newcastle in several age groups.

The club's first pitch was on what is now "The Limes" part of the hospital complex in Hartshill which in those early days was owned by the local GP. Eventually the club moved its base to land owned by a local farmer close to Lancaster Road in Hartshill, adopting the new name of Hartshill Cricket Club. The pavilion still stands, now owned and used by Newcastle-under-Lyme School.

In 1954 the club moved again, this time farther down the valley of the Lyme Brook to its current home, sited at the intersection of Stafford Avenue and Clayton Lane and taking the name of Hartshill and Newcastle Cricket Club. Following a funding grant made in 1957 by the Borough Council which enabled facilities to be improved and a perimeter wall to be built the club name was again changed, as a gesture of recognition to the Council, to Newcastle and Hartshill Cricket Club. The club also had a new pavilion which was opened in 1959.

The Clayton Lane ground was originally an area of marshland that was filled in and reclaimed and today it forms part of the land given into trust for the purposes of sport and recreation by the King George VI Playing Fields Association.

Newcastle played in the North Staffordshire and District Cricket League until in 1963 the club joined the breakaway league now known as the North Staffs and South Cheshire Premier Cricket League.

The club's first professional was Bill Boon, a bowler from Knypersley, followed by another bowler, Jack Norcup. Then C.H. Morley took a chance on a seventeen year old from Bradeley who helped the club win the league title. This young man was David Steele who went on to enjoy a successful career in county cricket. In 1975 he was in the England team that was pitted against Lillee and Thompson the legendary fast bowling Australians. He averaged over 42 and his efforts were rewarded by being awarded by popular acclaim the BBC Sports Personality of the Year award. His fame spread no little because a local Northampton butcher offered him a lamb chop for every run he scored against the Old Enemy. He duly prospered.

Arguably the finest professional that came to the club hailed from Lancashire. This was Arthur Sutton, who for many years was the opening batsman for Cheshire; and to this distinguished list can be added the names of Bob Bartels, Mike Moseley and Nassir Malik

Currently the club fields teams in the North Staffs and District League (Phoenix Competition) and the Stone and District Cricket League. In 2001 the Newcastle and Hartshill Junior Academy was formed to grow into one of the most successful in the county boasting over one hundred children playing in all age groups in the South Moorlands Junior Cricket League and the R. Cherry Kidsgrove and District Junior Cricket league.

Following what might be called a fall from grace the club is once again pulling its weight. This sleeping giant, promoted in 2013, is well on the way to recovery.

Norton Cricket Club was founded in 1857 and to confuse the unwary visitor plays its cricket in Smallthorne. The club owes its name to its origins, behind the historic Ford Green Hall, in the parish of Norton in the Moors, where it had its home for over fifty years. While at its first ground the club won its first significant title, the first championship in 1890 of the newly formed North Staffordshire League, by beating Tunstall in a play off.

Flooding from the Banky Brook was a constant nuisance through all these early years and finally in 1910, the club moved higher up the valley and achieved its second championship in the North Staffordshire League. The Heath family, local colliery owners generously financed the change of venue, thus establishing a long and lasting link between the club and the mining community. Several of the Heath family members played for the club alongside the workforce they employed.

During the Great War league cricket virtually ceased but some clubs, Norton among them undertook fixtures on an ad hoc basis for the benefit of servicemen on leave.

When league cricket began again after the war a second division was set up consisting of the second elevens of established clubs mixed in with new members. Anxious to maintain even opportunities the league management committee decreed in the same year that no professional should be employed.

This regulation lasted until 1925 when another second division was introduced, with promotion and relegation. In 1932 Norton suffered relegation to Senior "B": an indignity which was assuaged with immediate promotion the following year. "The seasons until the outbreak of the Second World War were not auspicious but our Senior "A" status was preserved" writes the club historian.

As everywhere the shades came down again over league cricket in 1939. On September 2nd Norton played the final match of the season with nine men as rapid mobilisation left the club short of players. The League did continue on a much reduced basis during the war with only one division operative. Even so difficulties particularly with transport made for hazardous administration and often fixtures were left unfulfilled. Final positions were calculated with an average system. Once again Norton kept the flag flying for the benefit of the local miners and the servicemen on leave.

After the war business was resumed as normal. Changes were afoot. In 1952 "Manny" Martindale, a celebrated West Indian Test cricketer became the club

professional, the forerunner of a host of famous names to adorn the club in the following few years. The graceful Frank Worrell took over in 1953, and became the first batsman to score 1000 runs in a league season in 1958 and followed this up with another 1000 runs in the 1959 season. Norton celebrated with him carrying off both the Senior (on three occasions between 1953 and 1958) and the Junior "A" (on two occasions between 1953 and 1958) championships. World record holder Jim Laker was next in line, succeeded by the acerbic Australian Cec Pepper and he was the professional when Norton took its place in the North Staffs and South Cheshire League in 1963.

In 1964 came the brightest star of all in this firmament: Sir Garfield Sobers whose stay at the club extended to three years bringing big crowds to the New Ford ground. Peter Gibbs writes in the 2014 Wisden the fact that players such as Sobers would be playing in the leagues "seems the stuff of make believe.....Today the stars are beamed to us by satellite as they follow a globetrotting schedule far removed from the colliery environs of Norton Cricket Club."

GARFIELD SOBERS
Captain of West Indies v. Australia 1965; v. England, 1966
Professional Norton C.C. 1964-65-67.

Sketched and Donated by :
Ald. H. BARKS, O.B.E., (Norton C.C.)

When Lord's relaxed the rules about county qualification and allowed overseas cricketers to play in the first class game Norton's heady days came to an end. In 1981, again to quote the Norton history "Norton's bubble burst and when in 1981 the NSSC expanded and an impure league was played with each of the 24 clubs playing each other once Norton found itself in the second tier."

The last thirty years have not been a tale of continued success but what is probably more important is that the club has survived when many of its fellow inner city clubs have gone out of existence. Much progress has been made in respect of providing opportunities for local players to enjoy the pleasures of our national game. There are six teams, a good playing area, permanent nets, an electronic scoreboard and full length covers.

All is in place for Norton to embrace the future with confidence and optimism.

NORTON IN HALES CC

The railway reached Norton in Hales in the 1870's when the North Staffordshire railway routed its Market Drayton line through the village – "Newcastle, Silverdale, Keele, Madeley Road, Pipe Gate (for Woore) and Norton in Hales" It took the village nearly 60 years to add a cricket club.

Norton in Hales was founded in 1928 as a village club to provide a sporting outlet for members of the local community. The club played at two earlier locations in the village before settling into its current home in the late 1950's. In the early days Saturday cricket was played on a friendly basis with just one team; but by the mid seventies this form of cricket was disappearing, leading Norton to join the new South Cheshire Alliance, competing against clubs from Shropshire, Staffordshire and Cheshire. At this time the club gained a reputation as a strong force in local knockout cricket – a format then, as now, frowned on by the purists but which was the forerunner of when the ECB decided on a move to a system of today's T/20 competition.

County based Premier League, the Alliance was broken up and in 1998 Norton in Hales joined the North Staffs and District League, gaining promotion within three years and taking the championship of Division One in 2000.

Promotion to the NSSCL in 2001 brought about the most notable on-field success in the club's history – possibly in the history of any local club. Immediately following promotion to the League, Norton in Hales topped Division One and then in 2002 went straight on to become Premier Division champions. During these times, Kevin Evans, late of Nottinghamshire and Imran Tahir, the Pakistani born test player, played as professionals at this ambitious club.

Sadly this quite unprecedented rise to the peak of local cricket was followed by an equally vertiginous fall. One year after its success in the Premier Division the club was relegated on the grounds of its inability to field a satisfactory number of junior teams and from that point the club slipped down the divisions, reverting to the status once more of a low tier village cricket club.

It could be argued however that the club's greatest challenges still lie ahead. In 2008 the pavilion was destroyed by fire, leaving the fate of the club in the balance. It took magnificent efforts from club members and the local community together with generous support from fellow NSSC league clubs to successfully construct a new building which all at the Shropshire club hope will provide a base for cricket to be played in the village for many years to come.

The club has run into hard times. A brand new pavilion has arisen from the ashes (literally) of the old one, with every desirable modern facility. But age and social mobility have both taken their toll. Older players have retired while the young ones leave in search of woods and pastures new. Neighbouring clubs have also proved a magnet to some. Professionals are a luxury long gone. The result is that a club bereft of its players loses its  lifeblood and Norton in Hales is now struggling to field two teams. The recent AGM seriously considered the possibility of folding the club

Despite these issues Norton in Hales will still be trying to rebuild in the 2014 season attempting to fight back from relegation to the Stone and District League. The emphasis is on recruiting and coaching young players with a view to building a new active membership. The cry is that for the moment at least the fight goes on! Its many friends in the NSSC family will wish them well.

The railway has come and gone – Long may the club survive.

OAKAMOOR CC

Oakamoor, where Churnet flows through a valley scarred by the works of the industrial revolution yet where some of sylvan charms remain. It was here, more specifically in the Cricketer Arms, that a group of friends decided to form a cricket club. The inspirational figure behind this ambition was John Davies, a muscular dystrophy sufferer, confined to a wheelchair, whose energy and drive were largely responsible for the foundation of Oakamoor Cricket Club.

The club in its first days was faced with the problem of having no ground of its own. The only way forward was to play away games only while the search for a home was carried out. Bolton Sports Ground in the village seemed the most obvious choice. This request was unfortunately refused.

The next port of call was a series of approaches to local landowners and the persistence was eventually rewarded when a local farmer agreed to offer a field on a rental basis. The landscape in the Churnet Valley is undulating to say the least and the land which the club had acquired was dominated by a steep slope. By dint of fundraising and the hard work of dedicated supporters the ground was levelled and a pavilion built. By 1979 the club was installed in its present home.

Friendly cricket was the order of the day for several seasons when club membership flourished. The induction into league cricket took place in an unusual fashion in that the way was led by the juniors, who became members of the South Moorlands Cricket League, where John Davies, who had played a leading role its creation, was for many years the secretary.

The club continued to grow and as the number of clubs playing simply league cricket was falling and fixtures were becoming more difficult to find. It was decided that the club should embrace league cricket and in 1986 it joined the Stone League, a move which proved a successful one.

In 1995 neighbouring Boltons Cricket Club proposed a merger with Oakamoor. After prolonged debate this was agreed and a new club was created: Boltons and Oakamoor Cricket Club. This led to the situation where two teams in the North Staffs and District League were playing at Bolton's ground, while Oakamoor's ground housed the Stone League's fixtures.

The Sports Ground was put up for sale in 2003 and with the help of grants and some vigorous fundraising an outright purchase was made and the job began of improving the ground and the facilities. At the same time the club reverted to its original name of Oakamoor Cricket Club.

Oakamoor celebrated its election to the North Staffs and South Cheshire League in 2006 by winning the Division 3A title. This victory predated further improvements and extensions and in 2012 a second pitch was laid down which meant that all teams could now play on the same site.

Several well-known players have turned out for the club. Staffordshire pace bowler Ian Worthington began his career at Oakamoor, and after spending some seasons with Caverswall, returned home where he still features in the second team (in 1999 in the Championship Division 3 competition Ian took a record number of wickets in a season - 99 at a record lowest average of 4.3 per wicket taken, these are likely to remain divisional records for many years to come). Other notable names include Kevin Barry, Ade Butters, Chris Prime, Alan Palmer and Anthony Bunn. Among recent professionals has been Shadab Jakati who has played in the IPL for Chenai Super Kings and Mohammed Ayub, the Pakistan Test Player

The club continues to progress and has achieved ECB Club Mark accreditation. It is served by many qualified ECB coaches and has a strong junior section which is a source of great pride to the club.

Martin Wolff, one of the founding fathers of Oakamoor Cricket Club nearly forty year ago, has seen the entire story unfold. He is now Chairman of the club.

OULTON CC

Since its founding in 1953 Oulton Cricket Club has always sought to combine a family atmosphere with high quality cricket. Currently based at the Spencer Copeland ground in Oulton Heath the O's have been permanent members of the NSSC League since promotion in 2006.

Affiliated to the Staffordshire Cricket Board Oulton first joined the Stone and District Cricket League with just one team. Frequent success brought several championship wins but not until the club could boast two teams could the club hope to attain elevation to the Premier League. By the early 80's they built up to two elevens yet still had to wait until 1995 before finally winning a place in the Premier League. Oulton then claimed the championship at the first attempt and was accordingly promoted to the North Staffs and District Cricket League, Senior "B". After another successful season the O's were promoted to the Senior "A" Section where having finished twice in third position they achieved their highest place in 2004.

Subsequently the club joined the North Staffs and South Cheshire League and won promotion to Division 1 under the captaincy of skipper Harish Patel finishing that season in a respectable fifth position. However next season saw the club suffer from no fewer than six retirements from the First Eleven, including the captain Patel, leaving a new look eleven contesting the 2011 season. Then Myles Coughlan took over the captaincy of a young side which despite being on paper well endowed with talent suffered relegation to Division 2 where it is currently competing.

Tom Spruce is now club captain and numerically the O's are as strong as ever, fielding three senior teams every week. In addition the club can boast a highly creditable junior division competing at several age levels.

Oulton can claim brilliantly conserved facilities with head groundsman and ex-player Shaun Howard taking superb care of both the playing and non-playing areas. Contributions made behind the scenes by club chairman Phil Jones and club secretary Brian Stretton and many other members have seen the club's facilities upgraded in recent times.

A new clubhouse and scorebox were erected in 2010 and 2011 in addition to new dressing room facilities. The clubhouse was lovingly put together by various club members while the scorebox will be named in the memory of the late Terry Malkin, a dearly loved member of the Oulton community.

The strength of Oulton Cricket Club today represents a glowing testament to the many people who have put in time and energy over the years to keep the club in existence through tough periods. Its wonderfully manicured playing area, skilful playing members and great atmosphere explain why this is a club loved by so many in and around the locality, be they cricketers or not.

PORTHILL PARK CC

Porthill Park Cricket Club's successes are recorded as early as 1895 as champions of the North Staffs League and then a remarkable period between 1906 and 1914 where 6 further championships were won. It's no coincidence that this successful period commenced when the great Sydney Barnes first played for Porthill Park in 1906. During the 9 year period he played for Porthill he took 893 wickets at an average of 5.28 and also managed to get in 23 test matches for England during his period with the club.

Porthill Park's Old County Ground in Wolstanton was first used to stage a Minor Counties Championship match in 1920 and it hosted a further 44 such matches up until 1966.

On joining the North Staffs and South Cheshire League in 1963 the club began the policy of working with local schools with the aim of unearthing and nurturing local talent.

By then one of Porthill's finest players, Dave Hancock, who had made his first team debut at the age of sixteen in 1956, was a regular member of the side. This talented left hander made his first appearance for his county just two years later and remained in the Staffordshire side over three decades. In 348 innings for Porthill Dave scored over 8500 runs, during which time he played some memorable innings. Many still recall his 110 against a Norton side including the great Garfield Sobers in 1965 as one of the best innings ever seen in the league.

During the 60's other Porthill players went on to represent their county. John Moore was one: a middle order batsman and a brilliant cover field who eventually became one of Staffordshire's leading coaches.

The 60's saw the club blessed with a gifted bowling attack: Peter Timmis, the professional, Stan Evans and Mick Ellsmore from the long gone Wolstanton Grammar School. There was a healthy influx of notable players during the late sixties and early seventies, including Peter Swanwick, a fine wicket keeper batsman and Keith Stride, one of the quickest bowlers on the scene at the time.

Peter Timmis' stint as the club professional came to a close in 1976. He was replaced in turn by Derek Nicholls, an all rounder, and then by Alan Mellor, an ex-Derbyshire left arm spinner.

With the reorganisation of the North Staffs and South Cheshire League Porthill Park found itself in the Second Division although gaining promotion in the following year after a protracted play off. The club languished in the lower tier of North Staffs cricket for many years. Finally the decision was made to increase the level of junior coaching and to form more junior teams. This move soon bore fruit as a group of fine young cricketers began to emerge. A team consisting among others of Neil Ellsmore, Dave Griffiths, Dave Cotton, Rich and Iain Powner, Paul Richards and Chris Howell revived the fortunes of the club by gaining promotion from the Second Division and bringing home the first silverware since 1949 by winning the Staffordshire Cup in 1997 and the Talbot Cup in 2000.

The professionals in this era included Scott Hookey, a big hitting Aussie who by virtue of his performances has become a legend within the club. Not least on account of a partnership of 104 in 10 overs with Andy Wagg. Andy scored one! Gordon Parsons, the Leicester seamer, also joined the club for several seasons as did Matthew Mott, an eighteen year old Australian batsman who broke the league record by scoring over 1100 runs in a season. Not surprisingly he was snapped up by Glamorgan as a club coach.

The current system continues to bring forward promising players: George Cairns, Ben Cotton, Zach Robinson, and Tom Mason are among those ensuring a promising future for the club.

Finally mention must be made of Porthill's wonderfully named seam bowler Brian Bailes. He should have been a wicket keeper.

Local cricket is the lifeblood of the game. Congratulations to the League on reaching its half century. Long may it thrive.

RODE PARK AND LAWTON CC

There are rumours of a document referring to a match between the Gentlemen of Cholmondeley Castle and the Gentlemen of Rode Park in the 1700's. If such unsubstantiated rumours are true this would set the date of foundation of Rode Park and Lawton CC back in the eighteenth century, placing the club in such esteemed company as Mitcham CC and Hambledon CC, clubs who were the cradle of the modern game. It has never quite lost its patrician past.

Rode Park and Lawton amalgamated after the Second World War with Rode Park chosen as the home ground. In 1963 the club was playing in the Cheshire Conference, a haphazard sort of league where clubs arranged their own fixtures at mutually convenient times. A breakaway league including Rode Park was formed in 1977 under the title of the Cheshire Competition. The club won the first division over three successive years from 1982-4 after which it joined the North Staffs and District Cricket League. The club was promoted to Senior "A" of the NSDCL, winning that division in 1999 but at that time the league was not a feeder to the next level, the North Staffs and South Cheshire Cricket League, Two years later the club again won the championship by which time the feeder system was in operation and the club was promoted to Division One of the NSSCL where it enjoyed several successful seasons.

With the overhauling of the leagues structure the NSSC League expanded into four divisions. Sadly, at the end of the 2010 season the club was relegated to Division Two where the club has remained ever since while it rejuvenates its programme of senior cricket.

Since 2008 the junior section of the club has grown from twenty eight players to over eighty; and these juniors will form the core of senior sides for many years to come as the club has no intention of paying more than one player as its professional, preferring to rely on home grown players and its ability to attract high calibre performers from elsewhere..

The club is one of the most picturesque in the area, set in the ground of the Rode Hall Estate and was voted the second best ground in the league in an article published in the Sentinel. As well as enjoying its beautiful location the club has undertaken over the years a large number of projects to ensure the high class of its facilities, which back in the early 1970's consisted of a home chicken shed, an away chicken shed and a teas cricket shed all of which were replaced by an old site office. This wooden structure lasted for many years and was later given fitted showers, a septic tank and proper toilet facilities.

In the mid 1990's the club became one of the first sporting bodies to be awarded funding from the National lottery. This, together with more funding from the Foundation for Sports and Arts, the club replaced the wooden structure with the present brick building. Increased junior participation led to funding from the ECB with the result that in 2009/10 the old concrete surfaced practice facility was replaced by a modern three bay artificial grass facility. The continued investment in facilities will help the club with its patrician history achieve its goal of returning to Division One.

SANDYFORD CC

Formed in 1874 Sandyford CC began life with a two year spell as the Oliver Cromwell Cricket Club. Various names were then knocked about a bit until the club finally settled on its present title in 1963, after spending more than twenty years playing as Meakins, named after the Tunstall potter Alfred and unconnected to the present club bearing the same name.

In and out of the North Staffordshire League in the early years of its existence – some time was spent in the North Staffordshire Combination League – the club re-entered the NSDCL in 1946, remaining there till 2004, when the first XI won promotion by right to the NSSCL.

The 30's and 40's were significant years for Sandyford: the club assumed and maintained its position in the league and made the move to the Shelford Rd ground where the club has played since 1940, Before that time Sandyford had played its games at a venue near Russell Rd and Wignall Rd, a site sold for building in 1935.

Although Shelford Rd has been home for Sandyford for more than 70 years, the club has been almost inextricably linked with issues surrounding ownership and tenure on the site. Over seven decades a number of false dawns on securing ownership and long term residency have come and gone, while numerous suggestions of a forced move have been seen off.

On the field probably one of Sandyford's greatest strengths has been to unearth and nurture young talent, the most notable being off-spinner Jason Brown and pace bowler Ken Higgs. Brown took 414 wickets in a thirteen year career with Northamptonshire and Nottinghamshire, during which he won a place in the England squad to tour Sri Lanka in 2001; while Ken Higgs, the only Sandyford player to graduate to Test cricket, took 71 wickets at an average of 20.74 in 15 matches for England, being named as one of Wisden's cricketers of the year in 1968.

It is this propensity for the development of young talent that sparked Sandyford's two most successful periods. In a spell of ten years from the mid 80's a team based on players from the local area enjoyed almost constant success in the NSDCL, winning the Senior A title and League Cup on numerous occasions, twice performing the double.

Likewise a team built on products of the club's junior section led an on-field resurgence after Sandyford was relegated to Senior B in both 2000 and 2002. In the decade that followed a Sandyford XIoften comprising ten players who began their cricketing life in the junior section made steady progress through the divisions. In 2010 Sandyford was promoted to the Premier Division of the NSSCL for the first time.

During this time it was not just the first XI that met with success. In 2010 the second XI won the Talbot Shield, the club's first NSSCL silverware while the indoor team has also reached the national finals on two occasions, the second of which was played at Lord's.

This era of playing success has been matched by a growth within the club, an expansion that saw the inauguration of a third XI as well as the expansion of the junior section to five teams, ranging from under nine to under seventeen

The club looks forward to a bright future.

SILVERDALE CC

Ralph Sneyd, the owner of Keele and most of Silverdale granted land around 1856 for a cricket ground to be built. 1879 saw the club move to its present venue by which time the North Staffordshire Railway was extending its line from Stoke towards Market Drayton, meaning that instead of being restricted to playing matches within walking distance, opponents as far afield as Leek and Crewe could be visited, The Sentinel was very dismissive about the team made up of miners but by 1869 it was beginning to win significant games; and by 1875 the club was able to engage its first professional – Thomas Trodd, a journeyman cricketer who had played for Surrey - a far cry from Silverdale in those far off days.

In 1889 Silverdale became a founder member of the North Staffordshire League and pursued an erratic career. The club finished at the bottom of the new league in 1894 only to carry off the championship in 1896 and 1897, success gained thanks to professional Job Lightfoot whose "lightning deliveries electrified opponents", producing a hundred wickets each season; and wickets that could well be described as sporting.

The ground preoccupied the club for many years. The original field had a ten foot fall and the ground had to be levelled and drained. By this time Ralph Sneyd's nephew (also Ralph) had given the ground to the club. A remarkable patron of the club in the early years of the century was the Grand Duke Michael of Russia, a cousin of the Tsar, living in exile in Keele Hall.

The 1920's saw more major projects. A new pavilion went up and then a tennis court, built, it is claimed, by striking miners. A formidable team in 1925 finished level with Bignall End at the top of the league and a play-off was subsequently arranged at Porthill Park: a two innings match spread over two days – which Silverdale lost.

Shortly after the Second World War the NCB bought the Sneyd Estates, ushering in a period of uncertainty for the club, reflected on the field in successive promotions and relegations. To some extent this was the result of the relative financial weakness of the club; but it also reflected the changing nature of the league as the wealthier clubs strengthened their teams by contracting world class cricketers while loyalty to a single club grew a more and more outmoded practice. For a twenty year period (1970's to 1990's) the club contracted no professionals and revelled in the nickname of "The Amateurs". One such amateur, Glynn Moore, has in 2013 achieved a personal milestone of 1000 league wickets for the club's first team. Glynn's first team debut season in 1987 gave cause for a great family and club celebration as he joined his father and three brothers in the same team and a few years later in scoring a century completed the unique feat of father and four sons all scoring a century in their career at the club.

The club failed by one single vote to gain entry into the North Staffordshire and South Cheshire Cricket League in 2003 after having won the senior section of the North Staffordshire and District Cricket League in the previous year: a decision heavily influenced by an adverse grounds committee report. This rejection spurred on club members to pursue a long-term partnership with Barclays Spaces for Sport, resulting in significant investment in the club's premises, practice and ground facilities. Inspections by the NSSCL officials have confirmed that the club is now well above the grounds and facilities minimum criteria for Premier Division cricket and the club now hosts many schools, district and junior county matches.

In 2008 the club gained the England and Wales Cricket Board Clubmark and now successfully runs three senior and five junior teams with ages ranging from under 9's to under 15's, reflecting the club's investment in the future. Junior cricket at the club is particularly strong now with widespread player representation at both district and county levels and field regular championship winning teams at all its junior levels. The second XI now plays its cricket in the Premier Division Section "B" finishing in 3rd place in 2013 with the first XI finishing the 2013 season in fourth place in Division 1 "A".

The story at Silverdale is one of continuous improvement on and off the field of play with players supported by a host of loyal spectators and volunteers the future looks bright for the club.

SNEYD CC

In 1927 the employees of Sneyd Colliery and Brickworks Company Limited formed a works team and one of the iconic local clubs came into being – Sneyd Colliery and Brickworks Cricket Club. It was in a sense a closed shop: to qualify to play "you needed to have a job at the works." Any problem with setting on professionals with this stricture in force was cleverly resolved – they were found a job at the colliery!

The club went on from its inception to become a dominant force in local cricket. It played throughout its existence on a ground that was in many respects a stereotypical industrial scene, tucked away in the looming shadow of the slag heap: "the grim smile of the Five Towns." Sneyd Colliery and Brickworks Cricket Club decided on a simpler title in the nineteen sixties, becoming simply Sneyd Cricket Club. As such it was one of the founder members of the North Staffs and South Cheshire League in 1963.

The club enjoyed many successful seasons in the new league, not least with its junior section. The under 18's topped the Kidsgrove League on no fewer than six consecutive seasons. Then, almost without warning, disaster struck in the seventies when the colliery was closed. The waves spreading from these revolutionary changes threatened to submerge clubs such as Sneyd who were linked so tightly to the pits. A vital artery was severed.

Compromises were struck for a while. A ground tenancy agreement was struck between the NCB and Stoke City Council affording protected status for the cricket club and a football club and league cricket continued, only to be threatened by another growing social change: that of vandalism. The changing rooms and scorebox were frequently targeted as was the pavilion and it was a devastating arson attack on the latter in 2003 that marked the looming demise The city council, who owned the ground, were unwilling to come to the club's rescue; and bereft of a home the club was forced to play all its games on an away basis. A merger was effected with Great Chell for a while in the early 90's but this time merger was not an option and the situation was in the end an untenable one and close of play was called for the last time in 2003. A great club, victim of cruel circumstance, passed out of existence.

The current league treasurer, Jess Hall, was for long a stalwart of the Sneyd club. He is a man who represents the old values of loyalty and selflessness without which no local club can live for long. In the forties, during the war years, as a boy of ten he watched his elder brother, a "Bevin Boy" play for the team. These were men in vital industries who were diverted from military service; and it was such players who kept some of the local teams playing at a time when so many young men were away.

Jess was ineligible to turn out for his beloved club and he played a season for the Michelin, however, the nationalisation of the coal industry changed the rules on eligibility and Jess could come home to Sneyd, where he remained as player and administrator until the club folded in 2003.

The young newcomer was predominantly a quick bowler and consistently topped the averages in the late 40's. Whenever possible he would travel back to Sneyd on Saturdays during his National Service days, determined to put in every effort for his club. Then a knee injury, sustained on the football field, necessitated two operations and his bowling days were done. Not to be deterred he concentrated on his batting and, as with his bowling, regularly carried off the honours. In the 1955 season he scored just short of a 1000 runs in a team that went through the season unbeaten and won the Senior "B" Section of the North Staffs and District League.

The club professional that year was Stan Crump, a name imprinted for all time on the local cricket scene.

No praise is too high for Jess whose dedication to his club as a player and an administrator was a constant. In the view of his many friends "he carried the club for years in both roles".

The roll call of memorable players who performed for the team over the years is impressive. Vince Lindo, an ex-Nottinghamshire player, "who bowled fast and hit hard" according to Jess, was certainly no local but having come to Sneyd as the professional, stayed on for five years and found a job at the colliery. Those notables who did come through the club were the Steele brothers, David (Northamptonshire, Derbyshire and England); John Steele (Leicestershire and Glamorgan, and then a first class umpire); Phil Bainbridge (Gloucestershire and Durham); and Andrew Brassington (Gloucestershire). A remarkable cast list for a small club.

Look carefully, though, and you will find the name of Sneyd in the out-of-season six-a-side indoor cricket league. The light still burns.

STAFFORD CC

Stafford Cricket and Hockey club was formed in 1864 although it seems that a town club had been formed as early as 1847. The club probably played its first games at Lammascotes before being offered a field at The Hough in 1899 that belonged to the grammar school. In August 1889 Lammascotes hosted a significant game against Burton on Trent whose team included the legendary fast bowler F.R.Spofforth who wreaked havoc on the local team in a low scoring game. Surprisingly this defeat seems to have infused fresh life into the Stafford club and the new ground at The Hough became their home for eighty four years.

Apart from the years of the two Great Wars, when many members were serving in the armed forces and cricket was suspended, the club looked south towards Birmingham for its cricket, eventually joining the Staffordshire Club Championship to ensure satisfactory competitive cricket for its members.

Towards the end of the 60's the activities of the club were inhibited more and more by industrial development and The Hough became an increasingly isolated sports field. In 1979 the club accepted an invitation from the well established NSSCL in order to enjoy a higher standard of cricket and it was decided that a move was necessary. Subsequently in 1984 the club moved to Riverway when GEC purchased its former ground, The Hough, from the then owners Staffordshire County Council.

The club then bought land on the site of the former GEC sports ground at Riverway along with an old RAF hut for just five pounds. Grants from Stafford Borough Sports Council helped fund a new grass square and a grant from the Lords Taverners enabled an artificial wicket to be put in which was operational by 1991. Club members carried out the necessary drainage work and the club purchased a further five acres from the council in 1995, taking out a twenty year mortgage. Two years later the club secured a low interest £5000 loan from the Stafford Playing Fields Association. After applying from 1991 for assistance the Foundation for Sports and the Arts the club finally secured a grant of £7800 and a five year interest free loan of £10000 in 1998 with almost all loans due to be paid back by 2004.

It was largely through efforts led by the late Brian Whitehead that the club was able to buy the extra five acres of land, thus creating space for two cricket pitches and several hockey pitches. When hockey turned to artificial pitches football and rugby moved in to use the facilities during the winter months.

Planning permission was granted in 1990 for the construction of a new clubhouse and even though cash was scarce members felt that the dream was turning into reality. In 1999 the club was awarded a two hundred thousand pounds lottery grant towards a new pavilion which was completed in the millennium year. This boasts six changing rooms, a members' lounge and a function room for members and guests.

Stafford Cricket Club has enjoyed unbroken membership of the NSSC which it joined on the league's expansion in 1979. Today there are five senior teams playing on Saturdays and Sundays and there is a thriving junior section.

2014 sees the club celebrate its 150th anniversary and there are exciting plans for the future which will see further development to its Riverway home providing an excellent sporting facility for the Stafford community and ensuring the future of the league's southern outpost.

STONE AND SWYNNERTON PARK CC

In 2007 Stone and Swynnerton Park Cricket Clubs merged to become Stone SP. Two clubs joining up to form a club with four senior sides playing on Saturdays in the North Staffs and South Cheshire Cricket League together with around two hundred youngsters and fourteen teams playing in the South Moorlands and the R. Cherry Kidsgrove and District Junior Cricket Leagues.

Early records show that cricket has been played in Stone since about 1845 and on the present ground on Lichfield Road since 1891. The first match there was played against Fenton in May of that year, Stone winning by one hundred and eighteen runs. The club also played at Aston, where the Second X1 used the ground which now is the home of Stone Hockey Club.

Several professionals were set on in the early years (some of them, it seems, quickly fired for myriad undisclosed reasons) and Edwardian cricket in Stone proved to be a lively affair: police constables were present at the ground to prevent crowd trouble. The committees comprised many of the town worthies, notably Pidducks the jewellers and the Johnson family, the latter taking on the payment to the various professionals. Remarkably such efficient management resulted in the luxury of two full time employees a groundsman and his assistant at a cost of three pounds per week. A luxury all clubs can now but dream of.

This was in the twenties; and one decade later Sir Ernest Johnson convinced the planning authorities that the ground should be classified as an open space, an act of foresight for which the club is grateful to this day.

In 1948, under the captaincy of H H Wood, Stone won the Senior "A"championship. Fred Taylor, an outstanding bowler and a local legend in his day, led the attack that season and in the following year broke the league record with a haul of 131 wickets

In 1976 Stone carried off the league championship and the Talbot Cup in the same season, the latter for the fifth time in twelve years. In 1979 another championship win was gained with a record number of points. Two years later the club won the Staffordshire cup in its inaugural year.

In 1950 the council started to build on three sides of the club which formed the ground as it is seen today. The Supporters' club presented the scorebox in 1952 while the pavilion was completed in 1961 and altered and extended again in 2008.

Stone has played host to many first class matches over the years. The first big occasion occurred in 1976 when Essex came to play Staffordshire in a Gillette Cup match. Thereafter came (in the renamed Natwest Trophy) Gloucestershire and Glamorgan. Another game in the competition featured Northamptonshire. Man of the Match here was Knypersley's own Rob Bailey, who came through the league system to play for his country. Rob scored 145 that day – but for his adopted county!

More counties came to Stone in the following years until Lancashire's visit in May 2004, the last first class fixture on the ground. There had been some stalwart performances in the twenty odd years without Staffordshire being quite able to clinch a victory.

At international level Stone was privileged to host Minor Counties fixtures against Australia, Pakistan and South Africa, matches blessed with good weather and sizeable crowds. Over 3000 spectators were present to watch the match against the Australians in 1993 when only a masterful all round performance from Paul Reiffel prevented a Minor Counties victory. In those golden years for Stone Cricket club supporters were entertained by such performers as Shane Warne, Inzaman-al Haq, Jacques Kallis, Wasim Akram, Hanse Kronje, Steve Waugh and Waqar Younis

Sadly, however, the last international touring party to visit Stone came in 1998, after which time changes to the first class fixture list put an end to games which represented such a bonus to small local clubs.

Meanwhile cricket has been played at Swynnerton Park since 1892 when the first recorded match with Stone shows a win for the home side of sixteen runs. The original pavilion was built in 1912 and narrowly avoided being damaged by a bomb which landed near the square during the Second World War. A piece of the shrapnel is on view at the club. The pavilion as it stands today was built in 2004.

Swynnerton Park, also the home of Staffordshire Gents has hosted matches for Staffordshire against Durham, Shropshire and Northumberland. In recent times many junior county sides have played at the ground. The merger with Stone in 2007 has ensured that cricket continues at this picturesque venue and has given many more opportunities for young players to develop.

It would be taking a risk to mention any player of Stone or Swynnerton for fear of omission. Every one forms part of the club's great history.

WEDGWOOD CC

Wedgwood (note the spelling: only one "e") was established as a factory team in 1942. At first the club played only friendly matches but seven years later it was playing league cricket in the Stone and District Cricket League where it remained until 1983 when it joined the North Staffs and District Cricket League. In 1992 relegation saw it returning to the Stone and District Cricket League where it played until it won back its place in 2005. In the following season the club became part of the expanded North Staffs and South Cheshire League where it now plays its cricket.

Wedgwood CC merged with Stanfields CC in 2009, taking that name. In 2012, at the request of the factory, the club resumed its original name, retaining the name of Stanfields in the Sunday team operating in the Stone and District Cricket League.

Wedgwood is the last so-called factory type team still playing in the area. In past years only Wedgwood employees were eligible to play in the side, a requirement that has long gone. But the Wedgwood Company has none the less always promoted the club which has ensured its survival and its members take pride in bearing the factory name.

It is interesting to note that players from past factory elevens are currently playing in the leagues, many former members of Wedgwood CC. Wedgwood is the last survivor from the teams of a bygone era: such as Michelin, MESC, Blythe Colours, GEC Stafford, Cegelec, Simplex Creda, Stoke M.O, Taylor Tunnicliffe, Shelton Iron and Steel, British Railways, Post Office Engineers, B.R.S, Rists, Johnson Bros, West Midlands Gas, City Works, Boltons, Meakins, Creda, Platts Tiles, Florence Colliery, Quickfit and Quartz, Mossfield Colliery and Sideway and SPW.

Wedgwood has claimed over the years the championship of the Stone and District League; the James and Tatton Cup; and of Division Three "B" in the North Staffs and South Cheshire League. During the mid 80's Wedgwood dominated the Stafford Knock Outs, winning the Dobson Cup and the Wood Shield twice. Several of its players have represented the Stone and District League team, occasionally providing the captain; and two club members have represented the North Staffs and District Cricket League. The under 11's represent the club's insurance for future seasons.

In 2011 "Mr Wedgwood" passed away: Cecil Leese, the last surviving founder member of the club, well respected throughout the leagues as a player and umpire. He had served the club as playing captain, secretary, chairman and president. He was associated with Wedgwood for sixty nine years and his memory will long be with all those associated with the club.

With Wedgwood Hall as a backdrop and surroundings of woods and fishing pools, a vast playing area and a fine clubhouse Wedgwood's ground must feature as one of the most picturesque in the county.

WESTON CC

Weston Cricket Club celebrated its centenary in 1997. Two years later the club historian and archivist, Alan Holdcroft, who sadly passed away in 2013, discovered an ancient newspaper in Nantwich museum which identified that the club was already in existence in 1875. Apart from the inevitable lacunae in the years of the two world wars the club has played without interruption, though in various leagues and changing venues.

To the traveller venturing north from the Potteries Weston is the first outpost in Cheshire. Open fields separated the two counties until a few years ago when the Co-Op, who owned great swathes of the land, sold out to developers and on land where the cattle grazed the Cheshire glitterati now enjoy their impressive properties overlooking the golf course.

Weston C.C has managed to survive these upheavals. The club once played at Toll Bar Cottage (now demolished); then, by permission of Lord Crewe, in the grounds of the Hall; and then in the hundred acre field stretching from Weston Hall farm to the Broughton Arms at Gorsty Hall. 1991 brought the need to move yet again after a new road was driven through by McAlpine.

Weston was playing Cheshire league cricket in the early 1900's and in 1932 joined the now defunct Scot Hay League. The team met with immediate success, winning the competition in the first season with 16 wins and only one defeat. 21 years passed before the club could repeat the feat.

When the Scot Hay League folded in the late 1950's the club were perforce obliged to settle for friendly cricket. A dearth of players proved a problem to further progress since only one team could be raised until a happy resolution was found by admittance to Division Two of the South Cheshire Alliance. Two titles were won outright in this competition as well as a shared top position with Norton in Hales.

Club membership had increased sufficiently by 1981 for the club to run two teams and two years later a successful application was made to join the North Staffs and District League... In 1985 the club progressed further and signed its first professional, Dennis Woodward.

Many will look back with nostalgia at their playing days on the ground set in the middle of a hundred acre field, protected from the cricket-watching cattle only by a slender electric fence which frequently gave a jolting tingle to the forgetful outfielder.

Despite the unique charms it was becoming obvious that that the ground, with its basic facilities, simply no longer came up to the growing expectations of today's game. The Barthomley by-pass road created an area between the new road and the existing A5020 and after careful consideration an approach was made to the Co Op to move to this area. This was agreed and grants were obtained to enable the club to build a new square and a brick pavilion with electricity and drainage. The first game on the new ground in 1992 was a fixture against the Derbyshire First Eleven.

Improvements on the ground brought higher playing standards to the club and Weston felt able in 2006 to apply for membership to the North Staffs and South Cheshire League, where the club was allotted a place in Division Two. A purple patch for the club began with winning the T/20 Cup in 2009; and gaining promotion to Division One a year later. The club professional at this time was Rajiv Kumar who gave five years sterling service, amassing over 1000 league runs each season.

The club's sojourn in Division One lasted only one season but cricket continues to thrive at Weston. A youth side was put into the Kidsgrove League as early as 1985 and this initiative has expanded to regular weekly coaching sessions for Weston's youngsters.

Finally a heartfelt tribute to Alan Holdcroft whose recent passing is a source of great sorrow to the club and to all who knew him, He was forty two years with the club, was first team captain for ten years, social secretary for 15 years and club secretary for 23 years and club historian into the bargain. He is remembered in the name of the club ground, dedicated to him – "The Alan Holdcroft Memorial Ground" - He typified the selfless spirit that is the heartbeat of a cricket club.

Weston Cricket Club provides a splendid example of what a village club, with limited resources, can achieve.

WHITMORE CC

In 1936 Whitmore Cricket Club was formed by a small group of local civil service and business people, playing their games in Keele Park before moving to the Whitmore ground. This ground was rented from the Cavanagh-Mainwaring estate to the rear of Peakes Farm opposite the Mainwaring Arms. Access was originally made across a very unsafe bridge spanning the Meese Brook, a source of water for the cricketers who were obliged to transport it to the pavilion in large metal buckets. No electricity or sewage facilities. Entry is easier today: via Bent Lane.

The pavilion acquired from Newcastle Golf Club survived until the 1950's; and older players have not very fond memories of splintered feet after contact with the wooden floor. After the game cricketers would retire to the especially reserved back bar in the Mainwaring Arms for ale and tea.

The first match on the ground was played on Saturday May 23rd 1936 against Stoke Municipal Officers. Whitmore were all out for 61 and the opposition for 15 – a fine start to the club's cricketing history.

The club played friendly cricket during the war years and in 1947 amalgamated with Butterton Cricket Club under the name of Whitmore and Newcastle Cricket Club. By 1963, when the North Staffordshire and South Cheshire League was formed as a breakaway from the North Staffs and District League, Whitmore was fielding a first and second eleven every Saturday and Sunday in matches throughout Staffordshire and Cheshire; and participating in midweek knockouts organised by Market Drayton and Woore.

When an invitation was received to join the now depleted North Staffordshire and District League the club took the decision not to accept. Funds were needed to buy a new clubhouse – which was opened in 1954, a brick construction with electricity and piped water; and which has been enhanced over the years into a welcoming as well as functional pavilion.

The club continued to thrive on a diet of friendly cricket until the early 80's when they joined the Shropshire Alliance followed by entrance to the Cheshire Conference League which became the South Cheshire Alliance. It was at this time that the club resumed its original name of Whitmore Cricket Club. It was at this time that the local vicar turned out for the club. – Strictly on alternating first and second eleven duties, always at home, availability assured if there were no Saturday marriages.

In 1997 Whitmore joined the North Staffs and District League, eventually opting to join the North Staffordshire and South Cheshire Premier Cricket League in 2002. 2013 saw Whitmore as Talbot Cup winners and playing in the Premier Division, which represents the highest standard ever attained by the club and pleasingly in the 50th anniversary of the League.

Cricket is played at many levels: Premier Division A and B; the Sunday Stone League; the Phoenix League during the week; and junior teams with ages ranging from under 17's to under 9's.

Several Whitmore players have played top flight representative cricket, including Danielle Wyatt, currently appearing in the England Women's team.

In December 2012 Whitmore was awarded the prestigious ECB Club Mark, a national award achieved only by reaching a high standard in community and club development, with a particular emphasis on junior cricket which Whitmore is proud to develop.

WOOD LANE CC

As the NSSC League celebrates its 50th anniversary it is an opportune moment to reflect on how a village cricket club became a member of the league surpassing the aspirations of its forefathers and its present day members and supporters.

In 1930 local footballers decided to form a cricket team to occupy their leisure time in the summer months. Early matches were played on Banker Wood, a farmer's field situated in the valley to the south east of the present ground. The names of these founders of the club are still remembered: George Clutton Snr, Jack Dewhurst, Harold Cook, Watson Oldershaw, Jack Statham, George Brayford, Caleb Johnson, George Turner, Isaac Durber, Bilston Cooper, Amos Hopwood, Reg Harrison and George Edge. Clutton's son George at 82 is still a regular attender and continues to contribute to the club. The newly created seating area is named after him and his friend and fellow supporter Eric Garvin. These two gentlemen are two among many to whom current supporters and members owe a great debt of gratitude.

George and Eric often reminisce about the 30's when players changed in a tent. They recall a notable achievement of those days when in a match against Stone Christ Church a Wood Lane bowler took all ten wickets for no runs. The tent was replaced by a timber pavilion maybe as a result of this feat.

After twenty years of recreational cricket the club entered a more competitive phase, joining the Scot Hay and District League. After four years the club finished as runners up and went one better the following year carrying off the League Championship.

In 1961 land at Megacre was offered to the club and with the help of grant aid from the Staffordshire Playing Field Association the new ground was developed. The name was changed at the same time to Wood Lane Cricket and Sports Club. Megacre was suitably shortened to give the ground the popular title of the MCG.

After several years of competing in the Stone League and the North Staffs and District League the club entered, in 2005, the NSSCL. Since that time the club has prospered on and off the field. Seven years of the club's membership of the NSSCL have been spent in the Premier Division. Between 2009 and 2012 the first and second elevens won all the available trophies, a feat achieved in the shortest span ever in the history of the league. However the highest achievement for the club was to become the ECB Premier League champions in 2011. The flag flying over the MCG was a wonderful sight for players, young and old, supporters and members; and recalling all who contributed to that success.

Many have played their part in these successes and in the respect duly gained; and to name every one would be an impossible task. Nonetheless it would be remiss not to mention the Norcup family, John, Steven, Doreen and Andrew. People like this are the lifeblood of cricket, helping their village club and its players and members to fulfil their dreams without seeking any reward. This family covers so many aspects: they provide opening bowlers for the first and second teams; the teas; and someone to build and repair.

Trophy cabinets and honours boards are wonderful prizes to cherish; but true success is measured by the opportunities offered by clubs like Wood Lane to those who want to undertake the challenges that cricket puts up in a competitive environment.

WOORE CC

Woore Cricket Club

There has been a cricket ground at Woore, situated in Shropshire – just – since at least 1896, on land originally attached to the Falcon Inn as part of its freehold. It was the building of the new railway from Stoke to Market Drayton which passed through nearby Pipe Gate which brought families anxious to escape from the smoky industrialised Potteries to the green fields of Shropshire and creating a ribbon of development over the mile and a half distance to Woore Square. The newcomers, able to use the railway to find opponents in Staffordshire and Cheshire, founded the cricket club in the village. The landlord of the Falcon reserved the right to provide all liquid refreshment, teas and seating; and his successors have duly prospered ever since.

Little recorded history of those days remains but one well known story has passed down. During the Second World War American troops based at nearby Doddington Park took the opportunity to play baseball on Falcon Field and offered to level the ground. Unfortunately the offer was turned down and to this day the notorious humps and hollows, with which visitors are all too familiar, prevail, giving the Woore outfield a unique character, as long off and fine leg will confirm. The open fields and picturesque setting combine to make this typical English cricket club a popular venue.

Woore Cricket Club is one of only two Shropshire clubs in the NSSCL. Until the 1970's friendly cricket was played and the club's reputation was built round the knockout competitions with solid silver trophies to be won. The matches drew sizeable crowds, no doubt swelling the coffers of the Falcon Inn. By this time the club had already nurtured a first class player: Albert Lightfoot, a highly talented all rounder, was a regular member of the Northamptonshire side and held the first class record for the sixth wicket for many years. At the Oval in June 1958 he and Subba Row amassed 376 runs, a mighty effort against a leading English county.

In the 1970's the club joined a league for the first time. The new South Cheshire Alliance brought together teams from three counties; the problem for Woore was the difficulty of fielding the required two elevens. This was solved when Tony Loffill brought a cohort of payers from the South Cheshire College in Crewe who made up a viable second eleven and ensured the club's participation in the new league. Some of these players subsequently played on for the club for many years.

The club performed well, buoyed up by local stalwarts such as the Baileys, the Rigbys and the Lawtons. The legendary Scott Cheshire joined at this time and it was under his stewardship, ably assisted by Bob Jones and an active ambitious committee, that seminal changes were effected at the club. The freehold of Falcon Field was purchased and a new pavilion and scorebox erected, work carried out for a large part by members and supporters. For the first time hot and cold running water, showers, changing rooms a kitchen and a bar were available.

By now, in 1987, the club was fielding three adult teams and hosting cricket weeks in conjunction with Market Drayton which attracted players of the calibre of the Cowdreys and the Bedsers.

Today Woore's players are drawn from a wide area. There is too a massive junior section, auguring well for the future with currently three members chosen at county level. Richard Oliver, Shropshire's present captain, began his cricketing days at Woore.

In 2014 the First Eleven are set to join the Second Division of the NSSCL for the first time. Friendly cricket will continue to be played however and Sundays will maintain the tradition of hosting local teams providing a home for those who want a more relaxing and recreational form of the game, just as in former days when the club was founded.

PRESIDENTS TROPHY
By Dave Yates

The League Cricket Conference has organised a knock out competition between its member League's since 1965.Our League was the first winner of the competition which in 1965 was sponsored by Rothman's of Pall Mall.

In recent years the League has had unprecedented success, in winning the trophy for the last five years.

This shows the level of skill and commitment shown by our players.

It is perhaps forgotten that the very first Captain of this team was our current Treasurer, Jess Hall.

The enthusiasm that Jess still continues to show to our League is amazing. Believe me no one looks forward, or dislikes the last match more than Jess. In fact he is miserable for a day or two after the game, just ask Joan.

Jess was a fine batsman in the days of uncovered wickets, but it is probably forgotten that he could also bowl.

In one season he topped the League bowling averages, however, during the close season Jess suffered an illness that caused him to stop bowling and from that point onwards he was simply a batsman.

Well done Jess, keep going.

I cannot name all the Captains that have led the side, but I have to give credit to David Fairbanks for leading the team for the last three years, when we have been dominant. His record speaks for itself and is testament to skill as a batsman and popularity within the League.

I must now mention one family who have contributed greatly to this team. That is the Lowndes family from Burslem. The family has provided no fewer than 3 Captains.

Firstly Paul, who captained the team in the early 90's and indeed, scored a century for his team. His elder son Steven then skippered for one season before having to stop playing for several years due to work issues.

Lastly, Paul's younger son Chris completed the hat trick and skippered the Team to winning the Trophy four years ago before handing over to David Fairbanks and as I said earlier, the rest is now history.

THE WINNERS, ROTHMANS OF PALL MALL TROPHY, 1965
THE LEAGUE TEAM — FINAL — GREAT CHELL, 22nd AUG., 1965

P. Shardlow   B. Griffiths   G. Hardstaff   P. Harvey   J. Broad   B. Coates   S. Wood
(Stone)   (Crewe LMR) (Crewe LMR)   (Stone)   (Longton)   (Sneyd)   (Crewe LMR)

J. D. Scholfield   W. Hall   D. F. Cox   G. Sobers   Nasim-ul-Ghani   J. E.V. Toney
(League Sec.) (Great Chell) (Crewe LMR)   (Norton)   (Longton)   (League
                      Captain   Chairman)

FROM UMPIRES' CLUB
TO
OFFICIALS' ASSOCIATION

Fifty years of service to local Cricket – By Derek Rowley

"Nostalgia - A sentimental longing for things of the past"

I was fortunate enough to be able to look back over the Minutes which I have in my possession for my review of the fifty years of our Umpires' group's existence. The number of Minutes in this archive is very extensive, but nonetheless, there are pretty big gaps in them. I do, however, feel that there has been move than sufficient material to furnish me with some fascinating reading and, hopefully enough to give a fair account of the way the organisation has evolved.   Fifty years is a long time and those early days make rewarding reading.

Our Umpire's group was born in 1964. A meeting was held at Great Chell Cricket Club on September 14th, 1964 following one which had been held with League officials on the matter of forming a League Umpire's Club. This was the first item for discussion at this meeting.   It was formally agreed to form a Club, its title being the North Staffs and South Cheshire Cricket League Umpires' Club.   The officials who were elected were:-

Chairman:	Mr. P. J. McColl
Vice Chairman:	Mr. T. W. Wooley
Secretary/Treasurer:	Mr. L. Stonier

If we believe that history repeats itself, then a reading of some of the entries in this book of the early Minutes of the Club will bear this out.

The first meetings established some things about membership. It was formally agreed that there need be no expansion of the Umpire panel, there were some 32 members available and it was felt that they were sufficient, both in number and competence to fulfil the needs of the League's matches.   Applications to join the Club were to be to the Secretary in writing and were to be subject to vetting via an interview (where now the Human Rights legislation?). It was noted that two applications for inclusion in the Club/Panel had been declined with no reason given!

A complaint had been received from an Umpire in the neighbouring North Staffs and District League to the effect that the new Panel was guilty of "poaching" its Umpires. This was refuted firmly. Even this early there was discussion on money. It was established that Umpires received expenses and not fees, since this had implications for tax payment.   This was last reinforced at a meeting 49 years later in 2012. The League was thanked for increasing the expenses from £1/0/0 to two guineas (£2/2/0)to cover the cost of bus fares to matches.

<table>
<tr><td colspan="2">UMPIRES, 1968</td><td colspan="2">UMPIRES, 1968</td></tr>
<tr><td colspan="2">First Division</td><td colspan="2">Second Division</td></tr>
<tr><td>1.</td><td>BATTERSBY, A. T.</td><td>17.</td><td>ALCOCK, R. W.</td></tr>
<tr><td>2.</td><td>BEECH, R.</td><td>18.</td><td>BOULTON, D.</td></tr>
<tr><td>3.</td><td>BUTLER, F.</td><td>19.</td><td>DAVIES, A.</td></tr>
<tr><td>4.</td><td>BUTLER, J.</td><td>20.</td><td>DUNNING, J.</td></tr>
<tr><td></td><td></td><td>21.</td><td>GIDMAN, H.</td></tr>
<tr><td>5.</td><td>HANCOCK, H.</td><td>22.</td><td>HARDWICK, Rev. J. W.</td></tr>
<tr><td>6.</td><td>HASSALL, A. J.</td><td>23.</td><td>HASSALL, S. B.</td></tr>
<tr><td>7.</td><td>HEATH, R.</td><td>24.</td><td>HUSON, A.</td></tr>
<tr><td></td><td></td><td>25.</td><td>JONES, C. A.</td></tr>
<tr><td>8.</td><td>HOFF, L. A.</td><td>26.</td><td>MORRIS, F. W.</td></tr>
<tr><td>9.</td><td>McCOLL, P. J.</td><td>27.</td><td>PEARSON, C. B.</td></tr>
<tr><td>10.</td><td>MAYDEW, T.</td><td>28.</td><td>POWNER, S.</td></tr>
<tr><td></td><td></td><td>29.</td><td>SANDERSON, G. A.</td></tr>
<tr><td>11.</td><td>MELLOR, J. A.</td><td>30.</td><td>WADSLEY, C.</td></tr>
<tr><td>12.</td><td>ROBINSON, G.</td><td>31.</td><td>WILKINSON, T. W.</td></tr>
<tr><td>13.</td><td>SIMPSON, S.</td><td>32.</td><td>PEPPER, H.</td></tr>
<tr><td>14.</td><td>SMITH, B.</td><td colspan="2">Supplementary : SCHOLFIELD, J. D.</td></tr>
<tr><td>15.</td><td>STONIER, L.</td><td colspan="2"></td></tr>
<tr><td>16.</td><td>WILCOX, D.</td><td colspan="2"></td></tr>
</table>

Umpires are NOT to exchange fixtures without permission of Hon. Umpires' Secretary.
Telephone : Stoke-on-Trent 55587

One casual note in the Minutes of 1968 refers to the programme of winter activities. These included a trip to see "My Fair Lady" in Birmingham as well as a proposed Ladies' Night. There were also visits by outside speakers to meetings held outside the season. Quizzes were a common occurrence and we find mention of the Lovatt Cup being won by the Club team with Roy Shallcross receiving the individual award.
A small thing which stands out as a possible indication of how times have changed and what some might see as a relaxation of "professional" standards. At a meeting in 1969, Umpires were explicitly instructed that it was not good practice for an Umpire to refer to a batsman by his first name!

At one meeting in the late sixties, it was agreed that the Club should be affiliated to ACU.   This was the principal, perhaps the only association which existed to educate and, thereby, raise the standards of performance of Umpires. This then heralded the teaching of courses for Umpires and – very occasionally – Scorers. We were now able to enter the era of fully qualified Umpires. Following a course of instruction, it was significant that the Chairman of the Club expressed his disgust that only 12 our of 32 Umpires had chosen to attend it.

A common theme found throughout the Minutes from 1964 to 2010 is criticism of the Umpires' Secretary. From Leslie Johnson to Ken Griffin we find cropping up complaints from Club members about their own appointments. Principally, of course, the complaints centre upon why they are not given fixtures of a greater significance. It is recorded that there was some unpleasantness surrounding the relegation of three Umpires to lower division matches, at the same time, a panel of 16 of the "better" men was set up. In 1966 it was established that a First Division Umpire (as it then was) must be prepared to stand in a Second Eleven game with a less experienced colleague. This is something which has been reiterated in very recent times as the shortage of Second Eleven Umpires has made itself obvious.

About three years ago we lost an Umpire because he had stood for about 10 games alone. In 1966 an Umpire complained of having to stand in six matches alone. In 1973 it was declared that no captain should ask an Umpire to stand at bowler's end throughout and, indeed, should he do so, measure would be taken against him!

As we look back over the years, we see another common denominator – the response to the Chairman's question - "Any interesting incidents gentlemen?" In 1967 only 4 batsmen were available to Leek's Second Eleven, the innings closing at fall of the third wicket. There had been a very unpleasant incident in a match at Great Chell involving a batsman's dismissal, "handled the ball". The point is, in each case, the Umpire relating the incident asked his colleagues whether his decision at the time had been correct. As much as anything, these little matters encapsulate the whole reason for the existence of the Umpires' Club.

1967 saw a very significant matter discussed. It expressed a truth still valid today. One of the Club members spoke to the effect that the then emergence into our cricket of the highly paid professional was having a detrimental effect. In that same season, we see an Umpire contacting the Umpires' Secretary to "cry off" three games because he found the pressure was now intolerable. This has been something repeated, albeit infrequently, over the ensuing years.

Some years ago a perennial issue was raised. Umpires saw the amount of money Clubs were now making and some resentment grew over what was seen as the view Clubs took of their Umpires. It was manifest in poor facilities for Umpires – they had nowhere designated as a dignified changing space, they had to queue for their teas and, too often, had to ask for their expenses. It has to be said that we have seen a great improvement in these things.

The year 1963 was seminal; the birth of the North Staffs and South Cheshire League. 2006 was a watershed of equal importance. In that year the North

Staffs and District League, one of the Country's oldest and most respected Leagues, ceased to exist. For this reason its Clubs responded to an invitation to amalgamate with the North Staffs and South Cheshire League.

For the Umpires' Club it was also a significant year. It was in this year, the year that would have been its 40th that the Club's longest standing Chairman died. Tony Davies had been a good servant. Anyone who writes any kind of a history, on no matter how trivial a thing, must surely tell the truth, otherwise there can be no purpose served. In line with this precept, it has to be said that Tony Davis was prescient in his deeply felt belief that for Umpires, amalgamation would lead to discord. Certainly, it proved to be so.

The meeting of 2006 which saw the first gathering of the two panels together at Bignall End was, at the very least, tense and, at worst, ill tempered. This was only to be expected. Change is notoriously difficult to manage successfully and when two groups come together, each with its own deeply embedded viewpoints and practices, suspicion is a natural outcome. So it proved. The existing panel feared that their positions would be usurped by the newcomers whilst the former District League Panel wondered whether they would be mere second class citizens or would they be able to receive fair play for their own service and expertise. Suspicion hung on, it has to be said, but it also has to be said that to the great credit of both sets of Umpires, it did not last for long. The existing members were not displaced and the newer colleagues got fairness. Over the past seven years matters have evened out well to everyone's credit.

"The objects of the Club shall be the holding of meetings for the
Discussions of matters of interest to Umpires, to improve the

Status of Umpires and generally to assist them in the discharge
Of their duties by the provision of educational or other facilities"

These words from the Objects and were written in 1964. They remain the same 50 years later. The Umpires' Club has now become the Officials' Association. The name change has no significance, other than being a reflection of changed times. What is important is the fact the Umpires "trade Union" is still an immensely valuable organisation. It always was and, all being well, always will be.

AN UMPIRE'S REFLECTIONS
By A. Glyn Forster.

I feel sure that I can say without contradiction that there is no one officiating as an Umpire today that was present at the birth of the League but if any such person existed he would have witnessed many changes in all aspects of the game.

Without any doubt there have been considerable and tremendous improvements in the playing facilities and in the standard of accommodation within the Club buildings. Gone are the days when a player would carry his equipment in a shopping bag with a larger kitbag for general use. A governing factor, influencing all Clubs today is finance, especially with the League now being "Open". Although there are those who decry this "Openness" it, at least, makes administration somewhat easier as previously, it was virtually impossible to police payment to players. It is recognised by players and Club Officials that Umpires play an integral part in the presentation of the game. It has always been essential that Umpires possess a very detailed knowledge of the laws and regulations governing the game and this is a feature that has seen considerable increase in recent years with the introduction of various types of cricket competition, such as T/20, Over 40's, 8 per side, and many National and Local Knock Out Competitions.

In the last few years Umpires have been privileged to enjoy improved facilities a feature that must continue for it is necessary to accept that there are "three teams" effective in any game and it is unacceptable to expect Umpires to tolerate cluttered and inappropriate changing facilities. Although the last few years have seen considerable changes in the way the game is played it can be expected that changes will continue in the future for various reasons, these include the findings of the current Eureka Initiative, instituted by the ECB it will be essential that Umpires make themselves conversant with any changes in the games presentation. Whatever the future may bring, it will necessary that Umpires strive to ensure that the game is played in the right spirit and in accordance with laws and regulations, To ensure that this is achieved all Umpires must be prepared to take the necessary action when there is any occurrence of indiscipline. Verbal admonishment at the time of the incident must be supported, when appropriate, by the accepted, reporting procedure. With the demonstration by all concerned, of correct and acceptable behaviour the aim of a season without any disciplinary hearings may well be achieved.

Encouragement should be given by all concerned to persuade individuals to take up the role of umpiring to ensure the game continues to be managed with acceptable and knowledgeable authority.

NS & SC PREMIER CRICKET LEAGUE
PAST and CURRENT OFFICERS

PRESIDENT:

	Year
J. S. Heath	1963 - 1967
J. E. V. Toney	1967 - 1980
B. McCardle	1980 - 1985
T. S. Bache	1985 - 1990
J. D. Scholfield	1990 - 1995
A. Fisher	1995 - 2000
L.J.Meredith	2000 - 2005
R. W. Flower	2005 - 2010
C.J.Hopkin	2010 -

HON. SECRETARY:

J.D. Scholfield	1962 - 1965
W.L.Johnson	1965 - 1969
J. Broad	1969 -
T. Pedley	1969 - 1972
L. J. Meredith	1972 - 2000
K.Tunnicliffe	2000 - 2004
A.Davies	2004 - 2006
D.Bloor	2006 -

HON. UMPIRES SECRETARY:

W. L. Johnson	1963 - 1967
L. J. Meredith	1967 - 1972
J. D. Scholfield	1972 - 1973
R. Heath	1973 - 1976
L. A. Hoff	1976 - 1994
L. G. Bennion	1994 - 2004
K. Griffin	2004 - 2010
E.A.Till	2010 -

CHAIRMAN:

J. E. V. Toney	1962 - 1966
B. McCardle	1966 - 1973
T. S. Bache	1973 - 1985
A. Fisher	1985 - 1995
C. J. Hopkin	1995 - 2010
J.S.Williamson	2010 -

HON. TREASURER:

H. Hampson	1964 - 1979
J.L.Handcock	1979 - 2004
J.S.Hall	2004 -

WELFARE OFFICER:

S. J.Colclough	2005 - 2007
T. Bailey	2007 - 2012
Mrs D.Shirley	2012 -

WEBMASTER:

C.Emery	2005 -

LEAGUE MANAGER:

K.Tunnicliffe	2005 -

ANNUAL DINNER AND PRESENTATION OF AWARDS
Grand Hotel Hanley, 12th October, 1963.
J. S. HEATH (President), C. G. HOWARD (Secretary—Lancashire C.C.C.)
J. E. V. TONEY (Chairman), D. F. COX (Captain, Crewe L.M.R., First Division
Champions), J. T. IKIN (Captain, Bignall End, First Division Runners-Up),
J. D. SCHOLFIELD (Secretary), A. WHEELER (Captain, Nantwich, Second
Division Champions), B. E. LOCKETT (Captain, Crewe L.M.R., Second Division
Runners-Up).

League Officers 2010
Jess Hall (Treasurer), Keith Tunnicliffe (League Manager), Russ Flower (President),
Chris Hopkin (Chairman) and Stuart Williamson (Vice Chairman).

LEAGUE FINANCES

"We now have the welcome stability of a sound financial basis" -Chris Hopkin commenting in his 2014 pre-season 'President's Message'

The 1967 table below shows over half of the League's income arising from the 12 member clubs annual subscription compared to broadly one third in 2013. The 2013 Accounts reflect the League's reliance on over half its income coming from the ECB Grant and sponsorship. Gate receipts for cup matches in 1967 were over one quarter of the League's income – in 2013 the return was just £145 – rules changes affected the moneys collected but it's more likely to be as a result of the significant wane in paying spectator interest over the fifty years. Fines of just under £3 were levied in 1967, very different from today's sum of £4,545.

Increases in admin expenditure are commensurate with support for 48 clubs and ensuring compliance with general legislation and ECB Directives. The appointment of a League Manager and increased Committee expenses now account for over 60% of expenditure. The League's cash/bank balances in 1967 would have provided cover for approximately one year's cricket and administrative operating costs whereas today (including an advance of sponsorship monies) the League has balances sufficient to cover eighteen months.

NORTH STAFFORDSHIRE and SOUTH CHESHIRE CRICKET LEAGUE
INCOME AND EXPENDITURE ACCOUNT FOR THE YEAR ENDED 17th NOVEMBER, 1967

EXPENDITURE

1966		£ s. d.	£ s. d.
102	Printing and Stationery		105 0 10
131	Handbooks		110 0 0
10	Scorebooks		13 1 11
26	Postages and Telephone		33 18 11
10	Hire of Rooms for Meetings		4 11 2
14	Insurance		13 13 0
8	Subscriptions		5 5 0
	Honoraria :		
63	Hon. Secretary	63 0 0	
5	Hon. Treasurer	5 5 0	
74	Players Awards	49 15 9	
2	Bank Charges and Cheque Books	1 15 0	
	Annual Dinner	264 2 0	
99	**Less** Received	215 17 6	
			48 4 6
13	Sundries		3 16 0
—	**Balance**—Excess of Income over Expenditure		107 3 5
£557			£564 10 6

INCOME

1966		£ s. d.	£ s. d.
	Annual Subscriptions :		
300	12 Clubs at £25		300 0 0
100	Sale of Handbooks		96 0 0
14	Sale of Scorebooks		14 8 0
	Public Liability Insurance	4 16 0	
—	**Less** Paid to N.C.C.A.	4 16 0	
1	Profit on Sale of Ties		1 19 5
5	Fines		2 18 0
44	Share of Talbot Cup Gates		64 19 5
—	Share of Talbot Shield Gates		7 13 5
	Share of Rothman Trophy Gates and		
31	Grants		76 12 3
62	Excess of Expenditure over Income		
£557			£564 10 6

BALANCE SHEET AS AT 17th NOVEMBER, 1967

LIABILITIES

1966		£ s. d.	£ s. d.
6	**Creditors**		8 2 0
	General Account as at 18th November, 1966	326 14 2	
326	**Add** Excess of Income over Expenditure	107 3 5	
			433 17 7
£332			£441 19 7

ASSETS

1966		£ s. d.	£ s. d.
1	**Debtor**		5 12 6
15	**Stock of Ties**		8 0 3
317	**Cash at Bank**		428 6 10
£332			£441 19 7

H. HAMPSON (Hon. Treasurer)

Audited and found correct :
A. CROPP HAWKINS, F.C.A. (Hon, Auditor)

Income and Expenditure Account
For the Year Ended 30 September 2013

	Budget 2014 £	Budget 2014 £	Actual 2013 £	Actual 2013 £	Actual 2012 £	Actual 2012 £
Cricket Income						
Annual Subscription		15900.00		15840.00		15840.00
Surplus at Annual Dinner		500.00		1179.30		1414.84
Cricket Balls		0.00		-228.02		-228.50
Fines		3000.00		4545.00		2900.00
Gate Receipts		100.00		145.00		108.00
League Cricket Conference		0.00		400.00		200.00
Transfer Fees		0.00		0.00		0.00
Additional TCS		0.00		0.00		124.00
		19500.00		21881.28		20358.34
Cricket Expenditure						
Handbooks			2828.00		2828.00	
Handbook Adverts & Sales	2200.00		-1110.00		-1027.00	
Scorebooks					0.00	
Committee Expenses	4500.00		4423.20		4288.02	
Umpires Association Expenses	600.00		375.00		527.00	
Competition Expenses	1600.00		1517.65		1057.25	
Webmaster Expenses	500.00		500.00		500.00	
Player Awards, Flags and Trophies	2000.00		1055.06		2167.91	
Ties	0.00		0.00		0.00	
Sports Equipment	0.00		0.00		128.00	
Longton CC Cockspur Cup	0.00	-11400.00	0.00	-9588.91	400.00	-10869.18
Cricket Excess of Income over Expenditure		8100.00		12292.37		9489.16
Administration Income						
Bank Interest		100.00	129.64		109.40	
ECB Grant		13500.00	13400.00		14050.00	
Sponsorship		9000.00	9062.33		5880.00	
Sundries - Raffles and Donations		250.00	407.00	22998.97	240.00	20279.40
		22850.00		22998.97		20279.40
Administration Expenditure						
Rent	1700.00		1650.00		1650.00	
Manager	17500.00		16706.16		16750.00	
Insurance	900.00		941.00		809.50	
Office Expenses	400.00		559.13		342.57	
Printing and Stationery	1000.00		599.95		757.38	
Postage and Telephone	500.00		493.18		494.78	
Publicity	500.00		500.00		400.00	
Subscriptions	50.00		40.00		40.00	
Donations and Sundries	200.00		160.10		50.00	
Celebration (50 Years) / Books	1000.00		1103.06		0.00	
Depreciation	50.00	-23800.00	17.00	-22769.58	69.00	-21363.23
Administration Excess of Expenditure over Income		-950.00		229.39		-1083.83
Total Surplus / Deficit		7150.00		12521.76		8405.33
SUMMARY OF SURPLUS DEFICIT						
Cricket Surplus		8100.00		12292.37		9489.16
Administration Deficit		-950.00		229.39		-1083.83
Total Surplus / Deficit		7150.00		12521.76		8405.33

Balance Sheet
As at 30 September 2013

	2013		2012	
	£	£	£	£
Fixed Assets				
Cost	3468.18		3468.18	
Less: Depreciation	-2732.18	736.00	-2715.18	753.00
Current Assets				
Sundry Debtors and Prepayments				
- Orange Payment included in 2010-11 expenses	0.00		0.00	
- Sundry Fines	390.00		390.00	
- ECB Payment	2500.00		2500.00	
Stock of Cricket Balls	420.50		420.50	
Stock of Ties	100.00		100.00	
Cash at Bank	46444.74	49855.24	27239.31	30649.81
Current Liabilities				
Sundry Creditors		-800.00		-800.00
J Whitfield - Paid in Advance		-6666.67		0.00
Cricket Academy		-4000.00		-4000.00
Scoring System		-2000.00		-2000.00
Total Assets less Current Liabilities		**37124.57**		**24602.81**
Revenue Reserve B/fwd		24602.81		16197.53
Excess of income over Expenditure		12521.76		8405.28
Revenue Reserve C/fwd		**37124.57**		**24602.81**

Report of the Auditor

I have examined the above Income and Expenditure Account and report
that they are in accordance with books and records presented to me.

I. A. Wheat
Auditor

Date: 1 November 2013

NS & SC PREMIER CRICKET LEAGUE LEAGUE RECORDS
E.C.B. PREMIER DIVISION A
(Formerly Division One - Section "A")

BATTING

			Year
Highest Team Score	380 for 7	Longton v Checkley	2004
Lowest Team Score	13 all out	Sneyd v Norton	1963
Individual Score	1408 runs	K.J.Barnett - Checkley	2004
Best Average	102.17	R.Kumar - Caverswall	2000
Highest Score	215 runs	I.Carr - Moddershall	2003
Fastest Century	45 mins (50 balls)	S.Afridi - Little Stoke	2004

HIGHEST WICKET PARTNERSHIP

1st	Wood Lane	269*	D.Brierley & R.Hassett v Burslem	2013
2nd	Audley	255	D.O'Callaghan & T.P.Singh v Porthill Park	2003
3rd	Knypersley	237	Q.Abbas & P.Goodwin v Little Stoke	2006
4th	Little Stoke	215*	A.Butters & T.Ecclestone v Elworth	1995
5th	Audley	187	A.Thomas & D.Bedson v Meir Heath	2007
6th	Porthill Park	210	M.Hole & D.Cotton v Betley	2005
7th	Porthill Park	142*	M.Mott & N.Gallimore v Elworth	1994
8th	Nantwich	123*	A.Newton & R.Wilson v Longton	1993
9th	Little Stoke	166	J.Ecclestone & G.Morris v Longton	2014
10th	Checkley	93	A.Carr & C. Price v Longton	2003

* Denotes unbeaten

BOWLING
Most Wickets in a Season

A.Clarke (Longton) (26 matches))	104	1996
Garfield S. Sobers (Norton) (22 matches)	97	1964
I. Tahir (Norton-in-Hales) (22 matches)	104	2002

Best Average

A.B.Jackson (Knypersley)	7.24	1970

All Ten Wickets in an Innings

R.T.De Ville (Longton) 10 for 37 v Leek	1969
I.Pearson (Leek) 10 for 47 v Elworth	2000
A.Johnson (Audley) 10 for 32 v Caverswall	2003
R.Shafayat (Barlaston) 10 for 41 v Porthill Park	2003

FIELDING
Best Fielding

P.R.Harvey (Stone) 23 catches (26 matches)	1980
M.Grimley (Knypersley) 21 catches (22 matches)	1982

Wicket Keeping

A.Coxon (Longton) 44 dismissals (22ct, 22st)	1970

Most Victims in a Match

K.P.Moore (Norton) 8 (5ct, 3st) v Great Chell	1980

YOUNGEST CENTURY MAKER

L.Banks (Hem Heath) 103 v Burslem (Aged 14 years 109 days)	2013

NS & SC PREMIER CRICKET LEAGUE
LEAGUE RECORDS
CHAMPIONSHIP - DIVISION ONE A
(Formerly Division One - Section "B")

BATTING

			Year
Highest Score	381 for 3	Kidsgrove v Meakins	2008
Lowest Score	16 all out	Elworth v Sneyd	2002
Individual Score	1415 runs	A.Chopra - Hem Heath	2005
Best Average	135.25	R.Nayyer, Leycett	1998
Highest Score	193no	I. Jawaid, Cheadle	2005
Fastest Century	41 mins (38 balls)	T.Azam, Moddershall v Leycett	1992

HIGHEST WICKET PARTNERSHIP

1st	Ashcombe Park	268*	R.Salmon & P.Hawkins v Sneyd	1995
2nd	Audley	234	D.Wellings & A.Johnson v Crewe RR	1994
3rd	Crewe RR	235	J.Maynard & I.Precious v Stafford	2006
4th	Barlaston	196	R.Berrisford & M.Stanyer v Burslem	1998
5th	Barlaston	171	N.Davies & R.Berrisford v Stafford	1984
6th	Crewe	186*	N.Singh & N.Lange v Sneyd	2003
7th	Bignall End	120	M.Horne & P.White v Porthill Park	1987
8th	Kidsgrove	140*	A.Green & D.Moors v Blythe	2009
9th	Bignall End	144	S.Billinge & L.Ikin v Burslem	2001
10th	Crewe	80*	N.Singh & M.Holt v Norton	2003

* Denotes unbeaten

BOWLING
Most Wickets in a Season

S. Gill (Barlaston)	125 wkts	2005

Best Average

B. Gessner (Sneyd)	5.9	1987

All Ten Wickets in an Innings

M.Ali (Buxton) 10 for 22 v Sneyd	1999
G.Singh (Wood Lane) 10 for 25 v Stafford	2006
C.Barker (Cheadle) 10 for 31 v Blythe	2009
I.Fazil (Norton-in-Hales) 10 for 35 v Crewe	2004

FIELDING
Best Fielding

S. Howle (Bignall End) 25 catches	2005

Wicket Keeping

Ikramullah (Norton) 52 dismissals (39 ct., 13st)	2002

Most Victims in a Match

M.Stokes (Caverswall) 7 (4ct. 3st)	2005

BATTING

			Year
Highest Score	408 for 7	Meakins v Weston	2006
Lowest Score	22 all out	Whitmore v Meakins	2007
Individual Score	1446 runs	R.Kumar (Weston)	2010
Best Average	103.28	R.Kumar (Weston)	2010
Highest Score	227 runs	I.Nazir (Meakins)	2006
Fastest Century	61 mins (56 balls)	I.Nazir (Meakins)	200

HIGHEST WICKET PARTNERSHIP

				Year
1st	Blythe	168	M.Grimley & M.Bailey v Silverdale	2007
2nd	Meakins	349	N.Kalleem & I.Nazir v Haslington	2006
3rd	Meakins	231	Z.Hussain & I.Nazir v Weston	2006
4th	Bignall End	179*	T.Mughal & S.Billinge v Meakins	2006
5th	Weston	181	R.Kumar & Q.Haleem v Whitmore	2007
6th	Ashcombe Park	137	A.Gondal & S.Proffitt v Caverswall	2008
7th	Silverdale	168	M.Moore & G.Moore v Hanford	2006
8th	Oulton	133	M.Dawson & T.Phillips v Oakamoor	2008
9th	Silverdale	74	G.Moore & Z.Lally v Caverswall	2009
10th	Oakamoor	103	I.Worthington & C.Jones v Ashcombe Park	2007

* Denotes unbeaten

BOWLING
Most Wickets in a Season

A.Butt (Newcastle & Hartshill)	86 wkts	2008
K.Daud (Silverdale)	86 wkts	2008

Best Average

M.Fayaz (Newcastle & Hartshill)	8.4	2012

All Ten Wickets in an Innings

A.A.Khan (Bagnall) 10 for 31 v Weston	2013

FIELDING
Best Fielding

R.Kumar (Weston)	23 catches	2010

Wicket Keeping

J.Jervis (Betley)	42 dismissals (29 ct, 13st)	2009

NS & SC PREMIER CRICKET LEAGUE
LEAGUE RECORDS
CHAMPIONSHIP - DIVISION THREE A

BATTING
			Year
Highest Score	333 for 3	Woore v Bagnall	2006
Lowest Score	21 all out	Woore v Norton-in-Hales	2009
Individual Score	1225 runs	K.Barnett (Bignall End)	2010
Best Average	90	I.Khalid (Bagnall)	2009
Highest Score	200no	R.Aslam (Woore)	2006
Fastest Century	66 mins (55 balls)	D.Pritchard-Porthilll Park "A" v Forsbrook	2008

HIGHEST WICKET PARTNERSHIP
1st	Endon	214	A.Bunn & M.Colclough v Wedgwood	2006
2nd	Hanford	221	I.Davis & A.Pickerill	2007
3rd	Stone SP	208	L.Cheadle & A.Butters v Hanford	2010
4th	Wedgwood	155	F.Patel & M.Edwards v Norton-in-Hales	2008
5th	Creda Stanfields	129	A.Palmer & N.Ali v Fenton	2006
6th	Fenton	129*	P.Farmer & G.Champ v Wedgwood	2006
7th	Buxton	102*	N.Smith & S.Hardman v Eccleshall	2006
8th	Woore	134	M.Hussain & A.Saunders v Eccleshall	2009
9th	Bagnall	76	A.Ravenscroft & P.White v Oakamoor	2009
10th	Norton-in-Hales	96	S.Ellwell & A.Bloor v Hem Heath/Forsbrook	2009

*Denotes unbeaten

BOWLING
Most Wickets in a Season
A.Raza (Bagnall)	104 wkts	2012

Best Average
A.Zaidi (Fenton)	5.47	2007

All Ten Wickets in an Innings
A.Zaidi (Fenton) 10 for 20 v Wedgwood	2007

FIELDING
Best Fielding
R.Gallichan (Eccleshall) 19 catches	2010

Wicket Keeping
A.Bailey (Endon) 39 dismissals (30ct, 9st)	2011

NS & SC PREMIER CRICKET LEAGUE
LEAGUE RECORDS
PREMIER DIVISION B
(Formerly Division Two - Section "A")

BATTING

				Year
Highest Score	357 for 6		Porthill Park v Betley	2004
Lowest Score	23		Crewe v Stone	1989
Also	23		Kidsgrove v Knypersley	1990
Individual Score	959		R. Hemmings (Audley) - 26 matches	1996
Individual Score	929		M.Womble (Longton) - 22 matches	1993
Best Average	92.16		I.Sutton (Little Stoke)	2001
Highest Score	242		J.McCarthy (Porthill Park)	2004
Fastest Century	53 mins		G.Davies (Kidsgrove)	1991

HIGHEST WICKET PARTNERSHIP

1st	Barlaston	297	A.Steele & A.Foster v Crewe	2002
2nd	Longton	262	B.Lucas & S.Pugh v Little Stoke	2005
3rd	Knypersley	226	C. Barry & M.Caddie v Sneyd	1985
4th	Stone	219*	S.Williamson & I.Banks v Elworth	1992
5th	Porthill Park	209*	J.McCarthy & G.Carins v Betley	2004
6th	Newcastle	161	P.Grocott & J.Hannon v Knypersley	1988
7th	Elworth	133	B.Williams & A.Stephenson v Ashcombe Park	1991
8th	Elworth	107*	P.Cross & C.Johnson v Bignall End	1996
9th	Knypersley	106*	P.Bates & I.Landon v Longton	2004
10th	Audley	90	L.Gibson & L.Kelter v Porthill	2013

*Denotes unbeaten

BOWLING

Most Wickets in a Season

A.Whalley (Longton)	77 wkts	2009
I.Reynolds (Norton)	77 wkts	2013

Best Average

S.Cartledge (Leek)	6.27	2002

All Ten Wickets in an Innings

S.Reynolds (Betley) 10 for 38 v Meir Heath	2004
R.Sherratt (Nantwich) 10 for 54 v Cheadle	1984

FIELDING

Best Fielding

O.Perry (Stone) 20 catches	2013

Wicket Keeping

G.Moore (Caverswall) 8 (all caught)	1994

NS & SC PREMIER CRICKET LEAGUE
LEAGUE RECORDS
CHAMPIONSHIP - DIVISION ONE 'B'
(Formerly DIVISION TWO - SECTION "B")

BATTING			Year
Highest Score	396 for 3	Blythe v Cheadle	2008
Lowest Score	9 all out	Stafford v Leycett	1986
Individual Score	1017 runs	A. Sutton (Stone)	2003
Best Average	103	N.Crump (Meir Heath)	2010
Highest Score	203 runs	D.Toft - Cheadle	2005
Fastest Century	60 mins	J.Boyle (Crewe)	2004
Six Sixes in an over		E.Riley (Bignall End)	1999

HIGHEST WICKET PARTNERSHIP

1st	Checkley	292*	M.Hall & R.Prince v Rode Park	2007
2nd	Kidsgrove	218*	A.W.Thomas & B.Dumbill v Stafford	1987
3rd	Cheadle	281	A.Shaw & J.Bullock - Sandyford	2007
4th	Cheadle	178	T.Walker & T.Clarke v Hem Heath	2008
5th	Cheadle	146	J.Welford & D.Cartlidge v Leycett	2008
6th	Cheadle	135 *	A.Alcock & M.Fox v Knypersley	2003
7th	Porthill Park	122 *	M.Farr & D.Billington v Norton	1992
8th	Bignall End	128*	A.Martin & R.Howell v Sneyd Gt Chell	1993
9th	Bignall End	89*	D.Edwards & N.Martin v Ashcombe Park	1995
10th	Sandyford	92*	D.Long & M.Skillcorn v Stafford	2013

BOWLING
Most Wickets in a Season

L.Steele (Barlaston)	109	1995

Best Average

P.Sutton (Ashcombe Park)	6.1	1987

All Ten Wickets in an Innings

D.Owen (Stafford) 10 for 17 v Crewe RR including Hat Trick	1991
T. Maguire (Barlaston) 10 for 45 v Sneyd	1984

FIELDING
Best Fielding

S.Saunders (Crewe RR) 22 catches	1990

Wicket Keeping

S. Johnson (Barlaston) 48 dismissals (19ct, 27st)	1996

Most Victims in a Match

D.Hollins (Burslem) 6 (5ct, 1st)	1986
G.Wilkinson (Sneyd) 6 (6ct)	1989
C.Bakewell (Barlaston) 6 (4ct, 2st)	1992
T. Slater (Norton) 6 (4ct, 2st)	1999

NS & SC PREMIER CRICKET LEAGUE
LEAGUE RECORDS
CHAMPIONSHIP - DIVISION TWO 'B'

BATTING

			Year
Highest Score	327 for 2	Oulton v Bignall End	2006
Lowest Score	30 all out	Oakamoor v Blythe	2007
Individual Score	1017 runs	I.Alcock (Ashcombe Park)	2013
Best Average	82.5	P.Wenlock (Caverswall)	2008
Highest Score	210 runs	J.Edge (Caverswall)	2011

HIGHEST WICKET PARTNERSHIP

1st	Oulton	241	M.Perry & D.Coughlan v Checkley	2009
2nd	Oulton	196	P.Malkin & D.Coughlan v Haslington	2006
3rd	Alsager	201*	A.Watkins & T.Blackwood v Betley	2009
4th	Oulton	183*	C.Whalley & A.J.Whalley v Haslington	2006
5th	Ashcome Park	178*	A.Byatt & S.Pheasey v Weston	2006
6th	Silverdale	116*	A.Green & L.James v Hanford	2006
7th	Norton	116	D.Hughes & L.Clowes v Oakamoor	2008
8th	Oulton	109	S.Harvey & M.Bates v Blythe	2007
9th	Bignall End	54*	M.Lawton & L.Salmon v Newc & Harts	2008
10th	Blythe	81	F.James & C.Grimley v Newc & Harts	2006

BOWLING
Most Wickets in a Season

M.Barcroft (Leycett)	102	2012

Best Average

J.Shenton (Silverdale)	5.5	2010

FIELDING
Best Fielding

A.Reid (Kidsgrove)	17 catches	2013

Wicket Keeping

G.Griffin 41 dismissals (40ct, 1st)		2010

NS & SC PREMIER CRICKET LEAGUE
LEAGUE RECORDS
CHAMPIONSHIP DIVISION THREE 'B'

BATTING   Year

Highest Score	326	Bagnall v Oakamoor	2006
Lowest Score	11	Fenton v Oakamoor	2009
Individual Score	699	P.Jackson (Moddershall "A")	2011
Best Average	63.8	S.Jodrell (Endon)	2011
Highest Score	177	N.Sargeant (Oakamoor)	2011

HIGHEST WICKET PARTNERSHIP

1st	Woore	259	D.Johnson & M.Dickinson v Hanford	2007
2nd	Alsager	136	A.Molyneux & R.Bason v Wedgwood	2008
3rd	Woore	155*	M.Bayliss & M.Razaq v Eccleshall	2006
4th	Oakamoor	144*	M.Carnwell & A.Sargeant v Endon	2009
5th	Wedgwood	196	G.Hall & C.Reeves v Oakamoor	2006
6th	Bagnall	82*	A.Hughes & M.Brazier v Wedgwood	2006
7th	Porthill Park "A"	90	R.Johnson & M.Cheadle v Eccleshall	2008
8th	Wedgwood	112	C.Reeves & I.Kavanagh v Swynnerton	2006
9th	Endon	63	S.Smith & T.Nadin v Stone SP	2008
10th	Stone SP	85	H.Bennett & D.Bradford v Oulton	2013

BOWLING
Most Wickets in a Season

| I.Worthington (Oakamoor) | 99 | 2009 |

Best Average

| I.Worthington (Oakamoor) | 4.3 | 2009 |

All 10 wickets in an Innings

| M.Austin (Endon) 10 for 19 v Woore | 2009 |

FIELDING
Best Fielding

N.Gilbert (Bagnall) 15 catches	2008
J.Litchfield (Bignall End) 15 catches	2013
P.Evans (Norton in Hales) 15 catches	2013
D.Robertson (Eccleshall) 15 catches	2013

Wicket Keeping

| D.Knapper (Wedgwood) 27 dismissals (21 ct, 6st) | 2008 |
| R.Melbourne (Bignall End) 27 dismissals (18ct, 9 st) | 2010 |

NORTH STAFFORDSHIRE & SOUTH CHESHIRE CRICKET LEAGUE CLUBS
HONOURS LIST 1963 – 1981

FIRST DIVISION		SECOND DIVISION	
1963	Crewe L.M.R.	1963	Nantwich
1964	Norton	1964	Bignall End (After play off)
1965	Norton	1965	Stone
1966	Longton	1966	Knypersley
1967	Norton	1967	Great Chell
1968	Longton	1968	Nantwich
1969	Longton	1969	Longton
1970	Longton	1970	Longton
1971	Great Chell	1971	Newcastle & Hartshill
1972	Longton	1972	Longton
1973	Knypersley	1973	Longton
1974	Leek	1974	Longton
1975	Crewe L.M.R.	1975	Longton
1976	Stone	1976	Leek
1977	Longton	1977	Leek
1978	Crewe	1978	Crewe
1979	Stone	1979	Nantwich
1980	Nantwich	1980	Stone
1981	Nantwich	1981	Cheadle

HONOURS LIST 1982 – 2000
DIVISION ONE

SECTION "A"		SECTION "B"	
1982	Knypersley	1982	Porthill Park
1983	Nantwich	1983	Caverswall
1984	Elworth	1984	Great Chell
1985	Newcastle & Hartshill	1985	Caverswall
1986	Crewe	1986	Knypersley
1987	Longton	1987	Audley
1988	Newcastle & Hartshill	1988	Betley
1989	Newcastle & Hartshill	1989	Caverswall

1990	Leek	1990	Nantwich
1991	Caverswall	1991	Burslem
1992	Ashcombe Park	1992	Porthill Park
1993	Cheadle	1993	Elworth
1994	Audley	1994	Stafford
1995	Knypersley	1995	Bignall End
1996	Stone	1996	Moddershall
1997	Moddershall	1997	Caverswall
1998	Little Stoke	1998	Cheadle
1999	Moddershall	1999	Bignall End
2000	Audley	2000	Crewe

HONOURS LIST 1982 – 2000
DIVISION TWO

SECTION "A"   **SECTION "B"**

1982	Cheadle	1982	Leycett
1983	Leek	1983	Bignall End
1984	Caverswall	1984	Barlaston
1985	Stone	1985	Kidsgrove
1986	Newcastle & Hartshill	1986	Bignall End
1987	Caverswall	1987	Newcastle & Hartshill
1988	Stone	1988	Barlaston
1989	Stone	1989	Ashcombe Park
1990	Ashcombe Park	1990	Porthill Park
1991	Cheadle	1991	Crewe
1992	Caverswall	1992	Porthill Park
1993	Caverswall	1993	Bignall End
1994	Stone	1994	Bignall End
1995	Caverswall	1995	Betley
1996	Elworth	1996	Newcastle & Hartshill
1997	Bignall End	1997	Barlaston
1998	Knypersley	1998	Cheadle
1999	Knypersley	1999	Bignall End
2000	Porthill Park	2000	Stafford

NORTH STAFFORDSHIRE & SOUTH CHESHIRE
PREMIER CRICKET LEAGUE CLUBS
HONOURS LIST 2001 – 2013

E.C.B. PREMIER DIVISION		E.C.B. PREMIER DIVISION "B"	
2001	Leek	2001	Audley
2002	Norton in Hales	2002	Audley
2003	Longton	2003	Checkley
2004	Longton	2004	Porthill Park
2005	Longton	2005	Stone
2006	Stone	2006	Leek
2007	Audley	2007	Porthill Park
2008	Moddershall	2008	Stafford
2009	Longton	2009	Wood Lane
2010	Little Stoke	2010	Knypersley
2011	Wood Lane	2011	Audley
2012	Leek	2012	Norton
2013	Leek	2013	Barlaston

CHAMPIONSHIP DIVISION ONE		CHAMPIONSHIP DIVISION ONE "B"	
2001	Norton in Hales	2001	Newcastle & Hartshill
2002	Little Stoke	2002	Meir Heath
2003	Stone	2003	Knypersley
2004	Burslem	2004	Elworth
2005	Barlaston	2005	Stafford
2006	Wood Lane	2006	Elworth
2007	Little Stoke	2007	Elworth
2008	Leycett	2008	Elworth
2009	Barlaston	2009	Barlaston
2010	Leek	2010	Norton
2011	Cheadle	2011	Cheadle
2012	Elworth	2012	Silverdale
2013	Meakins	2013	Stafford

CHAMPIONSHIP DIVISION TWO

2006	Bignall End
2007	Blythe
2008	Whitmore
2009	Oulton
2010	Weston
2011	J.G.Meakin
2012	Ashcombe Park
2013	Stafford

CHAMPIONSHIP DIVISION TWO "B"

2006	Ashcombe Park
2007	Norton
2008	Ashcombe Park
2009	Ashcombe Park
2010	Newcastle & Hartshill
2011	Checkley
2012	Leycett
2013	Kidsgrove

CHAMPIONSHIP DIVISION THREE

2006	Oakamoor
2007	Moddershall "A"
2008	Alsager
2009	Moddershall "A"
2010	Bignall End
2011	Eccleshall
2012	Bagnall
2013	Eccleshall

CHAMPIONSHIP DIVISION THREE "B"

2006	Woore
2007	Moddershall "A"
2008	Alsager
2009	Wedgwood/Stanfield
2010	Woore
2011	Hem Heath/Forsbrook
2012	Oakamoor
2013	Bignall End

NORTH STAFFORDSHIRE & SOUTH CHESHIRE
CRICKET LEAGUE CLUBS
TALBOT CUP
PREVIOUS WINNERS

Year	Winner	Year	Winner
1963	Norton	1990	Leycett
1964	Crewe LM R	1991	Leek
1965	Norton	1992	Leek
1966	Stone	1993	Audley
1967	Knypersley	1994	Stone
1968	Knypersley	1995	Longton
1969	Newcastle & Hartshill	1996	Stone
1970	Crewe LM R	1997	Stone
1971	Knypersley	1998	Longton
1972	Stone	1999	Moddershall
1973	Longton	2000	Porthill Park
1974	Stone	2001	Leek
1975	Leek	2002	Longton
1976	Stone	2003	Knypersley
1977	Bignall End	2004	Audley
1978	Stone	2005	Audley
1979	Longton	2006	Knypersley
1980	Leek	2007	Stone
1981	Cheadle	2008	Leek
1982	Cheadle	2009	Checkley
1983	Stone	2010	Wood Lane
1984	Crewe	2011	Elworth
1985	Newcastle & Hartshill	2012	Cheadle
1986	Newcastle & Hartshill	2013	Whitmore
1987	Cheadle		
1988	Leek		
1989	Audley		

NORTH STAFFORDSHIRE & SOUTH CHESHIRE
CRICKET LEAGUE CLUBS
TALBOT SHIELD
PREVIOUS WINNERS

Year	Winner	Year	Winner
1967	Nantwich	1990	Longton
1968	Leek	1991	Stone
1969	Longton	1992	Stone
1970	Crewe LMR	1993	Stone
1971	Longton	1994	Porthill Park
1972	Longton	1995	Stone
1973	Stone	1996	Longton
1974	Newcastle & Hartshill	1997	Crewe
1975	Knypersley	1998	Stone
1976	Stone	1999	Audley
1977	Leek	2000	Longton
1978	Norton	2001	Little Stoke
1979	Great Chell	2002	Moddershall
1980	Knypersley	2003	Moddershall
1981	Cheadle	2004	Barlaston
1982	Cheadle	2005	Elworth
1983	Leek	2006	Moddershall
1984	Stone	2007	Stafford
1985	Kidsgrove	2008	Stafford
1986	Audley	2009	Wood Lane
1987	Ashcombe Park	2010	Sandyford
1989	Stone	2011	Porthill Park
		2012	Porthill Park
		2013	Audley

NS&SCCL FIRST CLASS CRICKETERS SELECTED LIST

Qaiser Abbas   (Knypersley and Pakistan)

Jonathan Addison   (Caverswall and Leicestershire)

Shahid Afridi   (Little Stoke and Pakistan)

Mushtaq Ahmed   (Little Stoke and Pakistan)

Saeed Anwar   (Porthill Park and Pakistan)

R.Arrowsmith   (Crewe and Lancashire)

Mohamad Asif   (Barlaston and Pakistan)

Nathan Astle   (Longton and New Zealand)

Rob Bailey   (Knypersley and Derbyshire, Northants and England)

Phil Bainbridge   (Sneyd, Gloucestershire and Durham)

Herman Bakkes   (Cheadle and Orange Free State)

Kim Barnett   (Leek, Derbyshire and Gloucestershire and England)

R.Bartels   (Newcastle and Hartshill and Sri Lanka)

Joey Benjamin   (Stone and Warwickshire, Surrey and England)

Winston Benjamin   (Nantwich, Hampshire and West Indies)

Tino Best   (Leek and West Indies)

V.Brewster   (Norton and Barbados)

Mark Briers   (Nantwich and Durham/Leicestershire and Worcestershire)

Andrew Brassington   (Sneyd and Gloucestershire)

Barrington Browne   (Audley/Sneyd and West Indies)

Aakash Chopra   (Hem Heath and India)

Andy Clarke   (Longton, Stone and Sussex)

Jeff Cook   (Caverswall and Northants)

R.M.O.Cooke   (Knypersley/Essex)

Dennis F.Cox   (Crewe and Surrey)

Dominic Cork   (Betley/Porthill)

Brian Crump   (Little Stoke and Northants)

Cameron Cuffy	(Little Stoke and Surrey and West Indies)
Kevin Darlington	(Elworth and Guyana)
Vasbert Drakes	(Leek and West Indies)
S. Durani	(Great Chell and India)
Jack Dyson	(Newcastle and Hartshill/Lancashire)
Kevin Evans	(Norton in Hales and Nottinghamshire)
T. J. Peter Eyre	(Knypersley and Derbyshire)
Imran Farhat	(Porthill Park and Pakistan)
Russ Flower	(Little Stoke, Cheadle and Warwickshire)
Dave Follett	(Burslem, Middlesex and Northants)
Nigel Francis	(Longton and Trinidad)
Tony Frost	(Knypersley and Warwickshire)
Brian.D.Gessner	(Knypersley and Great Chell and Natal)
Peter Gibbs	(Norton and Derbyshire)
Ottis Gibson	(Leek and Durham/Leicestershire and West Indies)
Roy Gilchrist	(Great Chell and West Indies)
Trevor Goddard	(Great Chell and South Africa)
Wes Hall	(Great Chell and West Indies)
Dean Headley	(Leycett, Kent/Middlesex and England)
Claude Henderson	(Porthill Park and Leicestershire and South Africa)
Ken Higgs	(Sandyford, Lancashire, Leicestershire and England)
Alan Hill	(Little Stoke and Derbyshire)
Vanburn Holder	(Nantwich and Barbados/Worcestershire/West Indies)
Scott Hookey	(Porthill and New South Wales)
Mo Hussain	(Porthill Park, Stone, Leek, Barlaston and Pakistan)
J.T.Ikin	(Bignall End, Lancashire and England)
Andrew Jackman	(Longton and West Indies)
Brian Jackson	(Knypersley/Derbyshire)
Justin Kemp	(Little Stoke, Kent and South Africa)
Rajiv Kumar	(Caverswall, Whitmore and Kolkata Tigers)

Jim Laker	(Norton and Essex/Surrey and England)
Mick Lewis	(Longton and Durham and Australia)
Vince Lindo	(Sneyd and Nottinghamshire)
Albert Lightfoot	(Woore and Northants)
Nolan McKenzie	(Cheadle, Stafford and Guyana)
Alan Mellor	(Porthill and Derbyshire)
Dinesh Mongia	(Little Stoke and India)
D C Morgan	(Longton/Derbyshire)
Albie Morkel	(Leek and South Africa)
Morne Morkel	(Audley and South Africa)
John Morris	(Crewe and Derbyshire/Durham/Notts and England)
Matthew Mott	(Porthill Park and Victoria and Queensland)
Mahendra Nagamootoo	(Wood Lane and West Indies)
Imran Nazir	(Meakins and Pakistan)
Paul Newman	(Cheadle and Derbyshire)
Gordon Parsons	(Porthill Park, Leicestershire and Warwickshire)
C.G.Pepper	(Norton and Australia)
Andre Percival	(Elworth and Guyana)
Steve Perryman	(Longton , Warwickshire and Worcs)
Sonny Ramadhin	(Nantwich, Ashcombe Park and West Indies)
Ravi Ratnayeke	(Nantwich and Sri Lanka)
Dan Redfern	(Leycett and Derbyshire)
Wahab Riaz	(J&G Meakin and Pakistan)
Alan Richardson	(Little Stoke and Derbys, Middlesex, Warks &Worcs)
Mike Rindell	(Leek and Eastern Province)
Adam Sandford	(Moddershall and West Indies)
Keith Semple	(Elworth,Audley and West Indies)
Najaf Shah	(Ashcombe Park and Pakistan)
Ken Shuttleworth	(Sneyd and Lancashire/England)
TPSingh	(Stafford and Chandigarh Lions)
Jeremy Snape	(Kidsgrove and Gloucs, Leics, Northants and England)

Garfield S Sobers	(Norton and West Indies)
David Steele	(Sneyd, Derbyshire, Leicestershire, Northants and England)
John Steele	(Sneyd and Leek, Glamorgan and Leicestershire)
Peter Such	(Cheadle and Essex, Leicestershire, Notts and England)
Imran Tahir	(Norton in Hales, Moddershall, Kidsgrove and South Africa)
Bob Taylor	(Bignall End, Derbyshire and England)
Alfonso Thomas	(Longton, Audley and South Africa)
Lennox Tsotsobe	(Knypersley and South Africa)
Andrew Tweedie	(Longton and Natal)
Frank Tyson	(Knypersley, Northants and England)
Nasim ul Ghani	(Longton and Pakistan)
Mark Vermeulen	(Betley and Zimbabwe),
Roger De Ville	(Longton/Derbyshire)
John M.Ward	(Bignall End and Derbyshire)
Steve Waugh	(Nantwich and Australia)
Peter Webb	(Stafford and New Zealand)
Frank Worrall	(Norton and West Indies)
Danielle Wyatt	(Whitmore and England Women)

The League's Executive Board wish to thank our sponsors over the life of the League, your support is invaluable

Familyhomes4u - 2013 –

Waterworld - 2008 – 2010

Dukes Championship - 2007 – 2010

Readers Championship - 2006

Pipemaster Ltd - 1999 – 2006

John Davies Wholesaler - 1995 – 1996

MIC Financial Planning and Services Ltd - 1990 – 1994

Hanley Economic Building Society

The Sentinel

Bourne Sports

JPR Engineering Services

International Electrical Distributors Ltd

Essential Collections

ASC Financial Services

JSSports

JSW Insurance

JSW Accountants

Shark Cricket

Spyder Bats

Little Gym.